A Tiger by the Tail and Other Stories from the Heart of Korea

World Folklore Advisory Board

A Tiger by the Tail and Other Stories from the Heart of Korea

Retold by
Lindy Soon Curry

Edited by
Chan-eung Park

1999
LIBRARIES UNLIMITED, INC.
Englewood, Colorado

LIBRARIES UNLIMITED, INC.
P.O. Box 6633
Englewood, CO 80155-6633
1-800-237-6124
www.lu.com

Library of Congress Cataloging-in-Publication Data

Curry, Lindy Soon.
    A tiger by the tail and other stories from the heart of Korea /
retold by Lindy Soon Curry ; edited by Chan-eung Park.
      xxi, 128 p. 19x26 cm. -- (World folklore series)
    Includes bibliographical references and index.
    ISBN 1-56308-586-0
    1. Tales--Korea.   I. Park, Chan-eung.   II. Title.   III. Series.
GR342.C87   1999
398.2'09519--dc21
                                                        99-10669
                                                           CIP

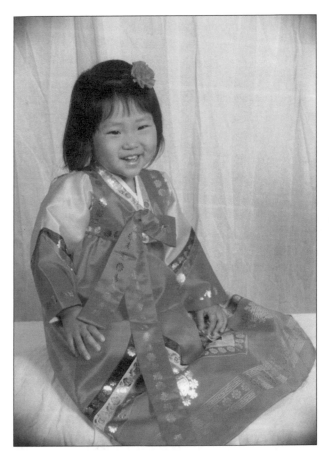

I dedicate this book to
my daughter,
Shannon,
so that it may help her
in her search for her
Korean heritage.

World Folklore Series

Folk Stories of the Hmong: Peoples of Laos, Thailand, and Vietnam. By Norma J. Livo and Dia Cha.

Images of a People: Tlingit Myths and Legends. By Mary Helen Pelton and Jacqueline DiGennaro.

Hyena and the Moon: Stories to Tell from Kenya. By Heather McNeil.

The Corn Woman: Stories and Legends of the Hispanic Southwest. Retold by Angel Vigil. Translated by Juan Francisco Marín and Jennifer Audrey Lowell.

Thai Tales: Folktales of Thailand. Retold by Supaporn Vathanaprida. Edited by Margaret Read MacDonald.

In Days Gone By: Folklore and Traditions of the Pennsylvania Dutch. By Audrey Burie Kirchner and Margaret R. Tassia.

From the Mango Tree and Other Folktales from Nepal. By Kavita Ram Shrestha and Sarah Lamstein.

Why Ostriches Don't Fly and Other Tales from the African Bush. By I. Murphy Lewis.

The Magic Egg and Other Tales from Ukraine. Retold by Barbara Suwyn. Edited by Natalie O. Kononenko.

When Night Falls, Kric! Krac! Haitian Folktales. By Liliane Nérette Louis. Edited by Fred J. Hay.

Jasmine and Coconuts: South Indian Tales. By Cathy Spagnoli and Paramasivam Samanna.

The Enchanted Wood and Other Folktales from Finland. By Norma J. Livo and George O. Livo.

A Tiger by the Tail and Other Stories from the Heart of Korea. Retold by Lindy Soon Curry. Edited by Chan-eung Park.

The Eagle in the Cactus: Traditional Stories from Mexico. By Angel Vigil.

Selections Available on Audiocassette

Hyena and the Moon: Stories to Listen to from Kenya. By Heather McNeil.

The Corn Woman: Audio Stories and Legends of the Hispanic Southwest. English and Spanish versions. By Angel Vigil. Spanish version read by Juan Francisco Marín.

Thai Tales: Audio Folktales from Thailand. By Supaporn Vathanaprida and Margaret Read MacDonald.

Folk Tales of the Hmong: Audio Tales from the Peoples of Laos, Thailand, and Vietnam. By Norma J. Livo and Dia Cha.

Contents

Section V
Tiger Tales

Section VI
Tall Tales

Preface

Once upon a time . . . at the end of the Korean War, near the naval base in Chinhae, South Korea, an American serviceman was walking along the street and saw a blanket lying in the gutter. He went to pick it up and found a baby crying and hungry in that blanket. He took that six-month-old baby girl to the Holt Orphanage. When she was four, she was adopted by a family and flown to their home in the United States. She was raised in Mt. Hood, Oregon, by this loving family. However, she always felt different from her adoptive family. When she went away to college, she explored many philosophies, took off on many adventures, spent time with lots of different people, and finally started to play the Celtic harp. A few years later, she became a professional storyteller, accompanying the stories with harp music. She married and amazingly ended up adopting a baby girl from Korea . . . and she lived happily ever after.

This is the story of my life—I was the girl the serviceman found in 1953. When I started to tell stories, the stories I liked best were those that helped me to get in touch with my many-faceted soul, which is both Korean and American. I was raised by a white, Protestant family, but when I graduated from high school and was on my own, I found that was not enough. So I began my search for who I am and what I was to become. Little by little, I was exposed to Korean and other Asian immigrants who befriended me and cooked for me. When I started to play the harp, I was attracted to some of the Korean as well as other Asian pieces, which beautifully lend themselves to the harp. Finally I learned some Korean folk and fairy tales that truly moved me. I was continually impressed that many of the stories I read from Korea showed strong, proactive women. This was helpful to me for I had many challenges to face, and these stories encouraged me to find my way in the world.

Asian friends, food, music, and stories helped me to accept the Korean parts of my being. I discovered what a rich heritage I have and became proud of how I looked and who I am. I write this book in the hopes it will help other Korean immigrants to feel more welcomed and finally adjust to life in the U.S.A. and to help others to understand and accept Korean Americans into their neighborhoods.

I chose stories for this anthology that demonstrate, for the most part, the power of love within families, relationships, and life stages—birth, marriage, and death. These are issues that concern me because of the circumstances of my life story. I have thought of my personal story as a story of compassion because it took the love and support of so many people to bring me to where I am today.

Folktales from each particular culture sprout and grow from deep within that society's collective unconscious to preserve its history and ideals. They help a group of people to develop socially as well as individually. That is why these stories have survived many centuries until they were finally written down in books for us.

Folktales from all countries have the same themes because humanity is the same throughout the world. We may look different, speak different languages, and practice different customs, but we all teach our children the same basic lessons: how to live, grow, and treat one another; and how to overcome obstacles and cope with life—the whole process of becoming a human being. Even some of the humor can be appreciated by all cultures. By learning one another's folktales, seeing the similarities, and being educated about the subtle differences in culture, we learn to understand each other and to embrace one another. Folktales show that no one group of people has the corner on wisdom and truth because we find some of the very same stories and lessons in every culture. With world travel and telecommunication, cultures are adopting mannerisms, language, and eventually customs of other countries.

There are many ways to interpret stories, and several themes may be present in each story. These themes can be a mirror to the culture, or, as with interpreting dreams, one can interpret stories by seeing all the characters in the story as parts of the self. I hope the stories I have chosen for this book will move you to think, feel, and understand more about yourself and others. Finally, remember that the purpose of stories is to communicate one heart to another.

Lindy Soon Curry

Acknowledgments

I want to thank my good friend, Judith Jacobi, a Jungian therapist, who helped me see the deeper and wider meaning of folktales. She gave me insight into why I was attracted to these stories and how they could help me in my search for meaning in my life.

I thank my editor, Chan-eung Park, for her dedication in making this collection of stories more compatible with the Korean culture than the other collections now in print.

I thank Richard McBride of the Korean Cultural Center (see page 111) for his generous help in providing most of the archival color images for the visual enhancement of the stories.

I thank Brian Barry, a contemporary artist, for contributing his fine works of art for the beautification of this book.

One special thank you to Kim Eui Kyoo for reading the manuscript and painting some special pieces just for this book.

I also thank Barbara Ittner of Libraries Unlimited for her assistance and encouragement to persevere with the writing of this book. I almost quit at one point, but she calmed my fears and inspired me to the finish.

And especially I thank my husband, David, for his support and tolerance of my writing schedule.

Tan'gun with seated white tiger, color on linen 75x95cm; Emille Museum, Seoul.
Courtesy of Korean Cultural Center.

Introduction—Folktales of Korea Retold

by Chan-eung Park

In every society, telling folktales is like lighting a timeless torch that illuminates the past as well as the present and future, and could there be a present or future without a look at the past? If the telling of folktales sheds insight into the world views of people from different places and times, what then is the relevance of just a handful of tales from a remote part of the world? They are of utmost importance because in this fast-globalizing world where the local interest of one nation directly affects that of another, we make efforts to understand and respect the values and thoughts of one another. In the tales of various cultures, we can celebrate finding common themes, plots, and characters, while humbly learning from their characters' differing paths of development. The Korean folktales selected for this volume are among the numerous stories transmitted orally from generation to generation. In recent decades they have been collected and recorded in writing as an important resource for studying the world views of the traditional Korea that has evolved over the last 5,000 years.

Jutting from the southeastern end of Manchuria, the Korean peninsula has since ancient times frequently been described by the native poets as the "brocaded embroidered rivers and mountains" (*kŭmsugangsan*). Framed by sandy beaches and the sparkling blue shores of the Pacific on three sides and dotted with numerous islands offshore, the land of Korea is blessed with an intricate mosaic of winding rivers that flow through the picturesque hills, dales, and majestic mountain ranges of the plains. Its geographic beauty has continually inspired a wealth of artistic, poetic, lyrical, and narrative traditions. Located at the crossroad of a cultural continuum in east and northeast Asia, the country has developed a most distinct pattern of religious rituals, philosophical thoughts, and artistic expressions. Since ancient times "when tigers used to smoke pipes," as the Korean expression goes, and throughout the area's dramatic history, Koreans have accumulated many fascinating myths, legends, folk songs, and tales. The history of Korea itself starts in myth in which the celestial beings and the inhabitants of the Earth are brought together to found an ideal kingdom that provides, as upheld in their foundation philosophy, "the maximum benefits to the greatest number of people."

The Buddhist Monk Iryôn (1206–1289) of the Koryô dynasty transmits the following foundation myth in his monumental *Memorabilia of the Three Kingdoms*. Hwanung, son of Hwanin, the heavenly guardian, descended to the Land of the Morning Calm (*Chosôn*) with the Earls of Wind, Rain, and Clouds. Out of compassion, he taught the humans 360 of life's matters—the number as many as the days in the lunar year. One day, he was visited by a bear and a tiger who wished to live as humans. Hwanung put them to a test in which the bear persevered, changing finally, into a woman. He lay with her, and Tan'gun, the first sacred ruler of Korea, was born. He ruled old Korea for 1,500 years before retiring as a mountain spirit. The spiritual, material, and ethical elements contained in the myth of Tan'gun presage the shaping of folktales that revere the sacred connection between this world and the netherworld, the totemic kinship between humans and animals, the worship of nature, the spirit of compassion, the teaching of humanity, and the priceless value of truth, goodness, and beauty.

Korean tales have thus come to manifest vividly the multifaced aspects of Korean cosmology, a blending of multiple spiritual ideologies: the animistic reverence for a nature in which everything animate or inanimate is a temple where spirits dwell; the Taoist practice of following nature's way in which a balance is struck between the *yin* and the *yang*, the dual principle of the negative and the positive; the Confucian ethical codes of filial piety and the way of an ideal social and political leadership; the Buddhist teachings of the unending chain of karma and incarnation; and, to top it all, there presides the omniscient and omnipresent Heaven. The complexity of the underlying thoughts, when woven into the fiber of folktales, finds amazing simplicity and humorous flavor on a most humanistic level. People of all physical, mental, and moral strengths are placed in challenging situations. Some encounter life's hardships or calamities. Some are faced with difficult moral choices. Some are challenged by spirits, goblins, and magical beings, and some, good heavens, by a hungry tiger on a lone mountain path. There are lessons to be learned—that things in life happen seemingly accidentally—but whether one survives or perishes is no accident. Those with discerning wit, goodwill, and superior virtues not only survive but often get handsomely rewarded, while greed, arrogance, or wanton desire invariably lead one to disaster.

About the Tales

The twenty-five folk stories in this volume are among the tales that continue to enjoy popularity among Koreans today. Some of them articulate themes and plot developments similar to the tales we are familiar with in the Western world. For example, the life of Kongjwi in *The Tale of Kongjwi* evolves in much the same pattern as that of Cinderella: the death of the mother followed by the father's remarriage, the stepmother's mistreatment, the assistance from guardian angels, the banquet, the shoe, and the happy ending. She is as beautiful and compassionate a protagonist as Cinderella, and the transition of her suffering to joy is as magical and magnificent as that of Cinderella. The tiger in *Sun and Moon* that eats a mother limb by limb is as violent and crafty as the wolf that gobbles up the grandmother in *Little Red Riding Hood*. In the Korean counterpart, however, Heaven intervenes to save the sister and brother by sending down the ropes. *The Toad Bridegroom* is easily identified with a character in the recent box-office hit *Beauty and the Beast*. Both stories uphold the moral that "looks can be deceiving," so "never judge people by the way they look." Both tell of the quest of a man to be truly loved and trusted and free of an evil spell, and both end with a dramatic metamorphosis from a beast to a prince once romance has been found and marriage is possible.

Not every tale, however, finds its Western counterpart as readily and neatly as the examples mentioned. The majority of the book's selections reflect and comment on the life in traditional Korea: its people's diverse situations involving money and power, filial piety, gender expectations, family relationships and social propriety, romance, marriage, aging, dying, the supernatural, and the natural. Usually, it is irony or a reversal of social expectations that highlights the moral lessons in the stories.

The Clever Wife is a good example of how a complexity of multiple themes is woven into a seemingly simplistic story about a man from an upper-class family who is discarded by his own father for not being able to learn how to read and write. But with the help of his clever and insightful wife of humble origin he not only learns to read and write but wins the first place in the royal examination. Traditionally, if you are a male from an aristocratic *yangban* family, your job would be to study literature, pass the exam, and be a government bureaucrat. Pak Hongjip's father banishes him because he falls short of fulfilling this expectation and thus performs an act of impiety to their ancestors and scars their family honor. Pak Hongjip, despite his sparkling intelligence and unusual ability to remember everything he hears, is irreparably illiterate. It is his own wife, a woman of humble origin, and not his male tutors of Neo-Confucian classics, who understands the fascinating dualism of literacy and orality, writing versus speaking, and reading versus hearing. She tells him stories, and he is curious to know her sources—curious enough to enter the world of literacy to see for himself! What a wonderful storyteller she must have been, and what a brilliant learning method is discovered in this great tale! How inspiring the idea would be if applied to the present battle against illiteracy in our own society!

The traditional Korean society has viewed women as subordinate to men, and few would argue differently. The readers of folktales, however, find reversing the socially assumed male superiority a pleasant twist when they encounter female characters with superior wisdom and determination who help their husbands succeed in life as in *The Clever Wife*. The story of *The Weeping Princess*, the fictitious version of the historical figures of Ondal and Princess P'yŏnggang of the Koguryŏ kingdom, is no exception.

The Weeping Princess, too, works a miracle on the husband of her choice, an abjectly poor, uneducated man who, though he has a heart of pure gold, is regarded by all as an idiot. By her magical hand, he is transformed into the best horseman and scholar her kingdom has ever had. In *The Value of Salt*, a woman's maternal wisdom helps her to eloquently defend her daughter's dignity from unending humiliation from her highbrowed in-laws. In the Neo-Confucian entrenched traditional Korea, you generally belonged to one of four social classes: the royalties; the aristocrats; the commoners; and lastly, merchants, artisans, craftsmen, and those considered social outcasts. The bride and the groom in *The Value of Salt* manifest actions and choices refreshingly revolutionary when the marriage does come to pass despite parental objections and social criticisms. An old proverb in Korea admonishes potential "upstarts" to "never look up at a tree if you cannot climb it." Under usual circumstances, intermarriage between the families of different classes was strictly forbidden, and the daughter of a lowly salt peddler is practically inviting woe on herself when she agrees to marry an aristocratic man. Her resolute mother sets the stage for remedy, however, when the in-laws are invited to make the moral connection between their own vainglory and the tastelessness of unsalted food they are given.

One of the discussions considered most timely in our society is about gender, and according to the current analyses, women are the victims of gender inequality in most parts of the world. In *The Tiger's Eyebrow Hair* and *The Magic Vase*, however, we encounter men victimized by their horrid, nagging wives. In both tales, magical or superhuman powers are what rescue these men: In the former, the wife is abandoned in sleep, and in the latter, she is blown away along with the house and all. The husband in *Yun Ok's Potion* has an equally intolerable temper, if not worse, that makes his wife, while seeking a remedy, risk her life in a series of dangerous encounters with a ferocious tiger. But the readers are given the possible reason why the man has become so embittered: He saw too much misery in the war. Instead of being abandoned or blown asunder, he is made reasonable again.

Since ancient times, the Koreans' reverence for proper human relationships found articulation in the Confucian ethics, namely, the five Confucian cardinal virtues: filial piety, loyalty for one lord, chastity for one man, respect for older siblings, and faith between friends. The virtuous ones observe the golden rules despite hardship and are rewarded in the end. Hungbu in *The Swallow Queen's Gift* is the model of a good brother who reciprocates his brother's mistreatment with unchanging love and respect and is rewarded with great wealth and happiness. The faithful servant in *The Pouch of Stories* saves his master from the ghastly plans of murder set by the angry spirits of stories the master had collected but had since forgotten. That stories have spirits in them and can turn against one who invited them but never remembered them is a story in itself. A lesson in propriety is accompanied by a slapstick comedy in the story of the pedagogue who sneaks into his *Honey Pot* before his hardworking students. In Korea, teachers are revered and even worshipped for their scholarly, ethical distinction. As a student, you are told never to commit the sacrilege of "stepping on the shadow of your teacher." But, alas, teachers must be human after all, and some of them are quite ordinary. The roles are reversed in the story, so the clever student teaches his teacher a lesson with wit and not a whip. The lesson in humility continues in *The Good Neighbor.* In a society where old age is respected and celebrated, a dispute erupts between an old man and a young man involving a tree shade. Unlike social expectation that the older you get the more generous you get, this old man is most disagreeable and petty. Defeated by the young man's clever wit, he ends up driving himself out of the shade, the home, and the village. But since he has not been a "good neighbor," no one ever misses him. A pair of allegorical fables included in this collection provide material for a study of the way of the world: *The First to Be Served* is a satire on how the power in this world is given to those who can effectively appear impressive, and in *Who Shall Marry Rat's Daughter?* our vainglorious craving for the greater and the higher is held to the mirror of self-realization.

Good lessons hardly cease to flow through the stream of humor in such tall tales as *The Wealthy Miser* and *The Fountain of Youth,* and what better ways of teaching modesty, humility, and moderation than packaged as humor? Sometimes humor is but a spice without apparent didacticism as in *Reflections.* A protagonist's joy of accidental encounter with success or savior is yet another sort of flavor worth mentioning: the nonsense-turned-success tale acquired in *A Tale for Sale* and the woodcutter's final tune that made the tigers dance instead of growl in *The Charming Flute.*

When it comes to romance, Korean storytelling has its share of "the tragic" in the form of death, reincarnation, or transformation. They say people in love conquer even the most trying hardships, and the princess in *Star-Crossed Lovers* does just that when she crosses the cold blue sea to her prince's kingdom. But, alas, their stars are crossed, as were those of Shakespeare's Romeo and Juliet. In *Across the Silvery Stream,* the famous constellation legend of the Altair and the Vega, romance is suspended, regulated, and not tragically ended.

Throughout the collection, the tiger is mentioned. Until before the Korean War (1950–1953), which massively destroyed the nation's forestry, Korea's majestic mountain ranges were home to what are known as Korean tigers. They were by far the most dreaded thing that travelers and wayfarers might encounter on deserted mountain paths. Spiritually, they have been revered and awed as sacred companions to the mountain spirits that are portrayed in numerous folk paintings. Thus, the Korean portrayals of tigers in folktales manifest the dualism of spiritual reverence and beastly abhorrence, of supernatural insight and natural appetite. They discern and help those with good hearts and at the same time lust after human flesh. In Korean tales this awesome, mysterious, and indifferent beast is often encountered by a Buddhist monk, whose holy profession has historically been questioned and satirized in times of religious corruption or upheaval. Before the gaping mouth of a tiger in *A Tiger by the Tail*, *Another Tiger by the Tail*, and *The Tiger's Grave*, the Buddhist practices in nonviolence are violently and mercilessly tested.

About the Storyteller and Storytelling

In this Internet world of virtual reality in which so many things come to us on a computer screen, we have for some time been less faithful in nurturing the traditional ways of learning, namely, reading and storytelling. More and more we rely on the computer's virtual thinking, writing, and speaking. Less and less our children have opportunities to learn life's valuable lessons from stories told by grandparents, parents, uncles, aunts, teachers, neighbors, and by one another. At this juncture, Lindy Soon Curry's contribution as storyteller is immeasurable. Born in Korea but adopted by Americans and raised in the United States, she brings to her storytelling for American readers her cross-cultural sensitivity, observation, and power of interpretation. As an experienced storyteller, she not only tells the selection in the way a story should be told but also provides readers with many insightful tips on storytelling. I hope *A Tiger by the Tail and Other Stories from the Heart of Korea* finds a wide audience, including our children, teachers, and interested storytellers so that we can create a global storytelling network.

About Chan E. Park (Editor and Writer of Introduction)

Dr. Chan E. Park is assistant professor of Korean language and literature at Ohio State University. She is also a performer and researcher of *p'ansori*, a traditional Korean storytelling art in stylized singing. In her numerous talks and performances around the nation and abroad, Dr. Park not only introduces Korean culture to her audiences, but also helps rekindle intellectual and public interest in storytelling, a powerful yet intimate tool of cultural and philosophical education.

Section I

Tips for
Telling Stories

Tips for Telling Stories

1. Read the story several times.
2. Tell it in your own words without looking at the book.
3. Read the story again to see if you left out some important points.
4. Tell it again, making it your own by:

   a. Changing the order of the story.

   b. Changing the beginning, ending, and transitions to make sense to you so that you can better convey the story meaning you want.

   c. Finding the repetitive elements of the story and building on them. Try not to say it exactly the same every time. Change the inflection or change one word. But, sometimes, if saying it exactly the same makes it more dramatic and more effective, then go ahead and do so. Repetition is good because it helps people to get back to the story if their mind has wandered. Whereas in the written form, readers can reread a story as much as they like, that cannot be done with the spoken word. If someone misses an important part of the oral story, that person may not get the meaning, and the rest of the story is wasted.

   d. Adding suspense by going into detail on conflicts and mystery.

   e. Using simple words. Remember people only remember half of what they hear. Use words that will evoke pictures in the listeners' minds. If you can picture the scene in your mind as you relate the story, the listeners will be able to also.

f. Using dialogue whenever possible—say the words the way that the characters would. You can use a slight accent or dialect, but not too strong because people will not be able to understand the story or will be distracted by the accent and forget to follow the story line.

g. Being consistent with vocal expressions and different pitch or tone of voice for each character's lines if they are used; and then you do not have to always state who said what because people will know by the tone of voice or body posture. This is one difference between the written and the spoken word, for in the written story one must always identify the speaker. Yet when a story is acted out in a play or in storytelling, one does not.

5. Make people "feel" and "see" the story. Don't just tell them the story, take them through each part of the story.

a. Use simple music or a song to set the mood.

b. What you wear adds interest. Since storytellers use simple staging, a costume that will help add to the images or themes of the stories is helpful to focus attention on the storyteller.

c. The tone of your voice and body posture will help them feel and see the story.

d. Invite the audience to participate:

1. Ask a question that the audience can answer. If an answer is not forthcoming, you can answer it.

2. Have them do the sound effects.

3. To help get people involved, have them sing with you.

4. Don't be upset or embarrassed if people don't participate since you, after all, are the performer in the story.

e. Use the appropriate gestures. Inappropriate gestures may distract from the words. When in doubt, don't gesture. You may map out the different parts of the story on stage and go to that area for that part of the story. You may sit or stand at different parts of the story as well as step forward or backward to emphasize different parts of the story.

f. Use props sparingly. Don't use too many props. They may distract people from using their own imagination in the story.

6. The power of storytelling is in helping people become so involved that they use their own minds to visualize the story for themselves.

7. You do not have to use all these suggestions. Try telling the story with one suggestion, then add another the next time you tell it. The most important thing about telling a story is to tell it in your own words in your own way. By telling the story, you give new life to it and keep the story alive for future generations.

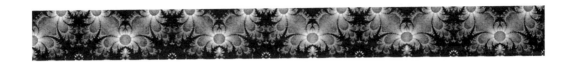

Section II

Stories Similar to Others We Know

The Toad Bridegroom

Long ago in Korea, the "Land of the Morning Calm," lived a fisherman and his wife. Every day the fisherman went to the lake to catch fish for dinner, but he noticed that the lake was shrinking smaller and smaller. He feared that it would dry up altogether.

One day he went to the lake and found that it had dried up, and in the middle of the lake bed was a big, fat, ugly toad. He right away accused the toad, "You have drunk up all the lake, and now all the fish are dead!"

"No, I did not. The lake was my home, and now I have none. Will you let me live with you? I will bring you good luck." "Fat chance!" The fisherman stomped home angry. He had no sooner arrived home when there was a knock at the door. His wife opened it to find a big, fat, ugly toad.

At first she was frightened, but then it spoke: "Kind woman, I have lost my home. May I live with you? I will bring you good luck."

When the wife saw the tears welling up in the toad's big eyes, she took pity on him and asked her husband. "We have no children. We don't even have a pet. Maybe he would make a good pet. Let him live with us."

When the husband looked into her big, brown eyes, he could not refuse her, so he said: "All right, we will try it. But if he causes any trouble, he's out."

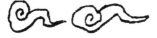

The wife served them each bowls of steamed rice and some *kimchee*, which is hot, spicy, garlicky, fermented cabbage and some clear noodles. The husband, thinking the toad would rather eat worms, went out to the garden and dug some up. The toad was very hungry and sucked up the worms loudly: "Slurp. Slurp."

The husband and wife at the other end of the table politely ate their noodles. "Sip. Sip."

The toad continued to slurp up his worms. "Slurp. Slurp." After he finished the last bite, he burped.

That toad ate so much that they teased him lovingly: "You are eating us out of house and home." But this was not true for no matter how much he ate, there was always rice in the rice bin and plenty of food. The husband and wife marveled at this and realized that the toad had brought them good luck.

Soon they did not think of him as a pet but started to care for him as they would their own son. He grew and grew, bigger and bigger until one day he was the size of a teenager!

The toad hopped over to his mother and said: "Mother, I need some clothes to wear. Please make me a *hanbok*." (*Hanbok* is the traditional Korean dress.)

"But I have never made one for a toad. I don't know how."

"Please, Mother, I need some clothes."

"I will see what I can do." She proceeded to sew up a fine *hanbok* of many colors, and when that toad put on the jacket and the pantaloons, he was the handsomest toad anybody had ever seen.

Then the toad hopped over to his father and spoke: "Father, I am ready to get married. I would like you to ask the rich man if I could marry one of his daughters."

"Now, Son, you know that your mother and I have grown to love you very much, but I don't think the rich man would understand. Perhaps I could find a girl toad for you."

"No, Father, I must marry one of the rich man's daughters. Please ask him." When the father looked into the big, bulging eyes of the toad, he could not refuse him.

The very next day he knocked on the rich man's door, and to his amazement he was welcomed in and was allowed to eat, drink, and smoke pipes with the rich man. They talked long into the afternoon, and the sun was going down, but he had not asked the rich man the question.

The Toad Bridegroom

Finally, he cleared his throat and spoke hesitantly. "O honorable one, I came to tell you that my son is of marriageable age, and I would like to ask if you would permit him to marry one of your lovely daughters."

"Son? I didn't know you had a son. Where have you been keeping him all these years? Has he been in another province going to school?"

"No, he lives with us. My wife made him a *hanbok*, and he looks so handsome."

"You can't be speaking of the toad? Marry my daughters!"

"Oh no, sir, only one."

"I know what you mean. How could you insult me thus? Of course, if he were a rich toad, I might consider. But he is a poor, lowly toad."

"But he has brought us good luck. He will do the same for you."

Clapping his hands he ordered, "Servants, throw this man out, and beat him."

The toad cried when he saw his father bruised and bleeding. "I had no idea that the rich man would treat you thus. I will take care of this matter."

That night the toad captured a hawk and tied to its claws a lantern. He then climbed a persimmon tree outside the window of the rich man. When he looked in the window, he saw the rich man sleeping. So he woke him with eerie sounds. The rich man went to the window and looked out to see where the noise was coming from, and up on top of the tree, he saw a light. From the light he heard: "I hear you have refused one of your daughters to

Art by Brian Barry.

marry the toad. If you do not let the toad marry one of your daughters, evil will fall upon your house, and you will have bad luck all the rest of your days. I will give you one day to reconsider." The toad let go of the hawk, and it flew away, but all the rich man saw was the light ascending into the heavens. The rich man thought that the Heavenly King had visited him and given him this warning, and he trembled with fear.

The next morning he called his family together and spoke to them of what had happened. He asked his oldest daughter, "Will you marry the toad and save the family?"

"No, Father, I can't. He is so ugly and slimy."

He asked his second daughter, "Will you marry the toad to save the family?"

"Have you smelled his breath? He eats worms. No, Father, don't make me."

Finally the youngest daughter spoke, "I will marry the toad to save the family."

"No, you are too young and innocent! Not my youngest."

"But, Father, I must save the family." The rich man knew he had no choice, so the wedding was arranged.

On the wedding day everyone was dressed in their finest, and then the music began. The vows were exchanged, and the deed was done. All the wedding guests shook their heads and wondered what was going to happen that night in the bridal chamber behind the screen.

I will tell you. The toad took off his jacket and folded it up and placed it on the chair. He took off his pantaloons and folded them up and placed them on the jacket on the chair. Then he lay down on the bed and waited for his bride. "Come, my beautiful bride, it is time. I want to kiss you."

She excused herself and went into the adjoining room. Taking a deep breath she prayed to the Heavenly King. Standing up she then took tiny steps to the bed—the tiniest steps that she could. She lay down on the bed—stiff. But nothing happened, so she opened one eye, and she saw the toad looking down on her and breathing. (Make cheeks bulge and contract.) She closed her eyes tightly.

Just then she heard the toad say: "Wait! First you must take that knife and slit open my back."

Horrified, she protested, "No, I may have been reluctant to kiss you, but I would never want to hurt you."

"Yes, I know, that is why I wanted to marry you. Please take the knife. Hurry, free me."

So she took the knife dutifully and stuck it into his back. "Zap!" To her surprise, it slid easily clear to the tail. From within a handsome prince stepped out and bowed to her.

"Thank you, my dear bride. I was under an evil spell from which only you could save me. Come with me now to my real kingdom."

He took his bride in one arm and his adoptive parents in the other. Together they went to live in his palace where they lived happily ever after.

But the bride always wondered what it would have been like if. . . .

Storyteller's Notes

In many Asian countries it is polite to burp once after a meal. It means that the food was so good that you ate it so fast that you got a bubble, and you have to burp. So on the count of three I have the audience practice their most polite burp. This is sure to break the ice with laughter.

I tell this story with lots of bowing to signify a change in speaker. Try pairing up and bowing to one another, and keep your eyes on the person as you bend over. Then try shaking hands. How do the different methods of greeting differ?

This story has a beauty-and-the-beast motif about a beast changing into a human after marriage. Sometimes it is the woman who is the animal, and she changes into a princess after marriage or a kiss. The theme of this story is not to judge a person solely by his or her outward appearance but to get to know the person on the inside as well. This is also a story of transformation depicting how people must change from their selfish, beastly selves and become real human beings to have good relationships. What is a "real" human being? What do you want to be when you grow up? Toads are many times a symbol of potency and sexuality. Therefore one may conclude from this story that sex can be either a frightening experience or a transforming and beautiful experience.

Why is it always the youngest child in folktales with the right answer? The youngest, especially in Korea, is not so bound by tradition and duty and is allowed to be more creative. You can also interpret the three daughters in this story as the first, second, and third idea or attitude. Perhaps one can think of all the daughters as parts of the self. We can peel off the layers of excuses and get to our real self.

The Fountain of Youth

There once lived a man and woman who had been married forty years, but everyone could see that they were still in love with each other. Their neighbors were amazed to see how happy they were even though the couple had no children. For this they pitied them because it was in those days considered a disgrace not to have children. "Who would care for us in our old age?" they asked and "Who would carry heavy loads for us?" The couple nonetheless remained cheerful and prayed that the Heavenly King would send them a child even in their advanced years.

One day the man went out to gather firewood when he heard a bird singing. When his eyes finally located the bird, it seemed to beckon to him. So he followed. It led him along a stream to a pool of water, and in the middle of the pool was a fountain shooting up.

The man was tired and thirsty, so he cupped his hands and took a drink of the water. It was so sweet and clear that he took another drink. It was the most refreshing water he had ever tasted. He felt invigorated and so excited that he ran home to tell his wife about this most wonderful discovery.

"Wife, you must come with me! I have discovered a new spring of water with the sweetest, most refreshing water in the world!"

"Who are you?" the wife asked of him.

"I am your husband! How could you not know!" he replied.

"Come to think of it, you do look like the young man I married when he was twenty years old."

When the husband looked into the mirror, he was amazed to see that all his gray hair had turned black, and all his wrinkles had disappeared.

"The water I drank must have done it. The bird must have led me to the fountain of youth. Come, Wife, so that you too may be young again!"

The two followed the stream to the fountain. The wife cupped her hands and took a drink. All her gray hair disappeared and grew back shiny, black, and long. She took another drink, and all her wrinkles disappeared—the skin on her face was smooth like a camellia petal. The husband and wife looked at each other in amazement. They held hands, and with renewed love and energy they practically skipped all the way back to their home.

Their neighbor happened to be looking out his window and saw the young couple going into the old house and mistakenly thought that strangers had moved in. Now this neighbor was a crotchety and greedy old man, especially since his wife died. He expected everyone to take care of him. He decided that he must introduce himself to this young couple, and so he went right over and knocked on the door.

"Hello. I am your elderly neighbor. I see you have just moved in. Since you are younger than I, you must respect me and take care of me. I want you to fix me dinner tonight."

"Oh, no. We are the same old couple who have lived here for more than forty years," replied the husband.

"No, you aren't. You can't fool me. The other couple had wrinkles and gray hair."

"We drank from the fountain of youth. That is why we look young again," explained the husband.

"You have been keeping this a secret from me? How could you! I want to be young also. Give me some of that water. Show me where it is this instant!" demanded the widower.

So the couple led the widower to the fountain. He drank and drank, but that was not enough. So he took his clothes off and dove into the water. The couple got tired of waiting for him, so they walked back home.

The widower did not return that night or the next day, and the kind couple began to worry about him, so they went back to the fountain where they last saw him. He was nowhere to be found. His clothes were still there beside the pool, but where was he? Then from the bushes they heard crying like that of a baby, "Waaa-waaa!"

That greedy old man had drunk so much that he had turned back into a baby!! The couple picked that baby up and took him home. Now they had the baby they had always prayed for. And they raised that baby to be good and kind and generous.

Storyteller's Notes

When I tell this story, I play water-sounding music on the harp for the fountain and strum the harp for the bird's voice. This is a very popular story with my audiences. I get requests for the retelling of this story many times. Sometimes children will guess and yell out that the old man turned into a baby again.

The theme of this story is not to be too greedy, but I like this story because everyone gets a second chance to change the outcome of their lives. What benefit would you get if you were to be younger? What age would you like to be? Do you have any regrets in your life, and how would you correct them?

The Tale of Kongjwi

In a small village in southern Korea lived a retired official and his wife. Although they were married for twenty years, they had no children. The wife went to the temple to pray for a child and bought expensive fertility medicines from her doctor. Finally one day she gave birth to a baby girl they named Kongjwi. The couple was very happy, but soon after the baby's 100-day birthday celebration, the mother died suddenly.

Kind neighbors helped to feed and take care of Kongjwi, and so she grew up to be healthy and beautiful. At the age of ten she was able to cook and sew and take good care of her father. But the father wondered who would take care of him when his daughter got married and moved away. He decided to marry the widow Pae-shi who lived with one daughter, Patjwi. As was the custom, the new wife managed all the household affairs.

From the beginning the stepmother and stepdaughter were jealous of Kongjwi's beauty and talents. They gave her the nickname Dirty Pig, and she was made to do all the work from sunup 'til late at night. Kongjwi was obedient and treated her stepmother with respect. One day the stepmother handed Kongjwi an old wooden hoe and told her: "You must weed the far field. Don't come home until it is finished." This was the field with the most rocks.

Kongjwi tightened her sash so that she would not feel so hungry for she knew that she would not be able to finish 'til nighttime and would have to miss lunch. The ground was so hard it broke her hoe in no time. "If I go home without weeding this field, I will be whipped and get no supper," she cried.

Suddenly a black cow appeared, and to her surprise it spoke to her: "My little girl, your kind deeds and brave heart have been noticed in Heaven. You shall be rewarded." As suddenly as the cow appeared, it vanished, and on the ground was a brand-new iron hoe and a basket of fruit. Kongjwi was able to finish weeding the field and ran home to share the fruit.

Nevertheless, the stepmother was angry: "You pig, where did you steal the fruit? Why didn't you come home in time to cook dinner?" That night Kongjwi went to bed with no dinner.

A few days later the stepmother told Kongjwi to fill the kitchen water jar. She filled it many times, but the jar remained empty. On the tenth trip to the well, a huge toad with bulging eyes hopped toward her and spoke to her, "There is a hole in the bottom of the jar, but if you place the jar on top of me, I will close the hole with my back."

"No, no!" protested Kongjwi. "I would rather suffer than risk breaking your back with this heavy jar."

The toad laughed and croaked: "I have lived 100 years! You deserve my help. Do as I say."

Knowing the jar was broken, the stepmother could not believe her eyes when she saw that the jar remained full of water. She wondered what magic was helping Kongjwi.

A week later Kongjwi was invited to her favorite uncle's wedding ceremony. Though Pae-shi was not invited, she decided to go anyway and take her daughter Patjwi with her. "Of course you may go, Kongjwi, but you must first weave forty yards of cotton material and polish the rice in the two large bags."

Kongjwi knew that the task was impossible, but she proceeded to spread out the rice on straw mats to dry. Immediately a flock of birds swooped down and pecked at the rice. She thought that they were eating the rice and tried to chase them away but to no avail. Then she grew so weary that she sat down and fell asleep. When she awoke, she saw the most beautifully dressed lady weaving on her loom. She had finished the forty yards of material and was just finishing a new dress. "I am the Weaving Maid from beyond the Silvery Stream (Milky Way), and I have been sent to help you. Here is what you must wear to your uncle's wedding feast," she said with a smile then disappeared.

Kongjwi started to protest because she remembered about the rice, but when she looked in the courtyard, she saw that the birds had not eaten the rice but had hulled and polished it. Kongjwi put on her new silk dress, and tying her hair with a ribbon she left for the wedding.

Kongjwi was happily humming a tune when a procession of people suddenly came by carrying the new governor in a palanquin. "Make way! Make way!" they ordered. It startled Kongjwi, and as she jumped off the road to kneel down, one shoe slipped from her foot and fell into the stream. She was miserable, but she continued on her way to her uncle's home with one stocking foot.

Her uncle was very pleased to see his favorite niece had finally arrived and served her the best food. But the stepmother turned red with rage and hissed in Kongjwi's ear: "Did you finish weaving the cotton and polishing the rice? Where did you steal that dress?"

Kongjwi explained to her that the Weaving Maid had helped her and given her this new dress, but the jealous woman fumed and plotted to punish her. The guests began to gossip about Kongjwi, and some praised her for her devotion to the family, but all wondered why she had arrived with only one shoe.

Meanwhile, the governor, who had seen Kongjwi beside the stream, noticed a bright red shoe floating by. Thinking it might belong to the beautiful girl, he ordered a servant to fetch it. "Go find the owner of this shoe," he instructed. The governor's messenger ran along the country road asking everyone he met and then at last reached the house of the wedding feast.

Patjwi called out: "I recently lost a shoe! It must be mine." She grabbed the shoe and tried to squeeze her large foot into it but could not—it looked so ridiculous that everyone laughed.

An elderly woman called out, "Look, there is a young maid who has lost one shoe." The messenger asked Kongjwi to come forward, and when he saw that the foot slipped easily into the shoe, he bowed low and instructed her to ride in the palanquin to meet the governor.

The governor was immediately taken by her modesty and sincerity. He was so completely captivated by her beauty, filial obedience, and charm that he asked Kongjwi's father if he could marry her. Her father begged the governor to reconsider and informed him that his daughter was from a poor, humble family and did not have the education to become the wife of such an important person. Yet the governor would not change his mind and married Kongjwi.

They lived a very happy life and were blessed with three sons and two daughters. Kongjwi's fame spread far and wide, and her womanly virtues are still remembered throughout Korea.

Storyteller's Notes

The Cinderella motif is one of the most common in all cultures. Sometimes it is the boy, "Cinderfella," who is mistreated and has to do all the work. Everyone feels persecuted at some time in their life, or they feel that they are the only one doing all the work, or they resent others telling them what to do. As one gets older, more responsibilities and work are expected, but the story says that if you work hard and take responsibility, you will reap the reward. In a very realistic sense, you will also know how to take care of yourself because you have been practicing the tasks for a long time. They become good habits that are easy to do and free you to pursue other goals.

When have you felt things were unfair, and what was the outcome? Can you think of an example when help came at the last minute when you didn't think you could take unfairness any longer? Notice how Kongjwi had help from many sources: a black cow, a frog, the birds, and the Weaving Maid.

Sun and Moon

There once was a woman whose husband died and left her with a boy and a girl to care for. She was lucky, however, because she worked for a kind family, cooking and cleaning. Her mistress one day gave her a basket of buckwheat pudding to take home to feed her children. The woman was very happy and walked home humming to herself.

Just then a tiger jumped out of the bushes and roared at her. She was very frightened, "Please leave me alone for I must get home to my children."

The tiger cared nothing about her children, "I demand that you give me the buckwheat pudding to eat, or I will eat you up!" The woman threw him the basket and hurried home as fast as she could. She did not go far for the tiger ate the pudding in one gulp and caught up to her and roared, "I am still hungry. Give me more to eat!"

"I have nothing more for you," the woman pleaded.

"What are those things dangling from your shoulders?"

"My arms? Surely you don't want them."

"Yes, I do. Give them to me, or I'll eat you up!"

So the woman let the tiger rip off her arms, then she ran home as fast as she could. But she did not get far for the tiger came after her again.

"I am still hungry! Give me your legs to eat!"

"No, please. How will I be able to get home to my children?"

"You can roll, can't you? Give them to me now!"

The poor woman let the tiger rip off her legs then started to roll in the direction of her house. The tiger came after her and ate the rest of her up in just a couple of gulps.

Now you would think that the tiger would have been satisfied, but no. He thought of the children and what a nice dessert they would be. So he dressed in the woman's clothes, stood up on his hind legs, and carried the now empty basket on his arms. He soon came upon a house and peeked in. When he saw the children, he knocked at the door.

"Children, open the door. Your mother is home now."

The boy and girl knew there was something wrong for their mother never came home that late after dark, so they had locked the doors. The voice did not sound right either, so they replied, "Mother, why do you have such a scratchy voice?"

"Because I have been yelling at the crows to keep them away from the garden all day. Now please open the door, for I am tired and cold out here," the tiger replied in as sweet a voice as he could manage.

"Please put your hand in through the window that we can make certain that you are our mother," the children requested. The tiger wrapped his hand in cloth and stuck it through the small crack. The children were not fooled, so they asked one last question, "Why is your hand so rough?" As the tiger answered, the children ran out the back door to hide and get in a safe place.

"Because, my dears, I have been washing clothes all day, and they are chapped. Now I must demand that you open the door at once! Enough of these silly questions!"

But the children did not answer for they had climbed a tree in the back of the house. The tiger banged and banged on the door, but when there was no response, he tore down the door. The children were not in the house, but he saw the back door and went out to search for them. In the backyard was a well in which he saw the reflection of the children.

"There you are. Come out of the water right now for you will be soaked and get sick." The children could not help but laugh at this foolish tiger. The tiger upon hearing the laughter looked in the direction from whence the sound came and spied the children in the tree. Since tigers do not climb trees he had to ask sweetly, "My darling children, how did you get up there?"

"We climbed up," they replied, "but since you do not climb trees, you must get some sesame-seed oil from the kitchen and spread it on the trunk of the tree—as much as you can. That will help you to climb up."

The stupid tiger spread sesame-seed oil on the trunk of the tree, but when he tried to climb up, he could not get a hold and kept slipping down and falling on his backside. After many attempts he was angry and roared: "Tell me the truth or you shall be punished. How can I climb up this tree?" The children had been instructed by their elders to always tell the truth or they would not be considered good people, so they told the tiger to take the ax and cut notches in the tree trunk to make steps up.

As the tiger cut notches, the tree shook, and the children trembled with fear. As the tiger started to climb up the tree gripping the notches, the children's hearts pounded louder and louder. They climbed higher and higher to get further away from the tiger, but soon they heard him panting. The smell of his fetid breath came near and nearer.

In desperation they cried out, "We pray to you, oh Heavenly King, please save us from this horrible, vicious tiger!"

The Heavenly King sent down a "golden chain" that the children grabbed onto and were pulled into Heaven.

The tiger cried out also, "Heavenly King, send me a golden chain and save me for this tree is about to break."

The Heavenly King sent down a rotten rope, and when the tiger grabbed onto it, it broke. He fell to the Earth, and his blood splattered all over the field of buckwheat. It is said that the roots of the buckwheat plant are red to remind us of how the Heavenly King saved the children from the terrible tiger.

But the story does not end there. The story goes on to say that the children were very happy in Heaven. They were rejoined with their mother, who was put back together. The children played and danced and sang. The Heavenly King told them that it is not good that children play all the time—they must have a job to do. So he made the boy be the moon to shine on the Earth at night so that people may see their way. The girl he made be the sun to shine on the Earth by day and warm the Earth and make all living things grow.

She was so beautiful that everyone stared up at her all the time. She was shy and modest and did not like people to look at her all the time, so she made herself shine brighter and brighter until, to this very day, people must not look at the sun without protecting their eyes.

Painting by Kim Eui Kyoo, Ansan City, South Korea.

That is the story of how the sun and the moon were made.

Storyteller's Notes

Children love this story with all its gore and suspense for everyone has been in some scary situation that causes one's heart to beat faster. Even in ancient times parents had to leave children, and often there were those who were not to be trusted. Then again, mothers must leave their child in the care of others for them to grow up and mature. All parents instruct their children about what to do in dangerous situations. They are admonished to be careful of "wolves in sheep's clothing." Also, if one gives into evil once, it will be easier and easier to do so in the future.

This is a story where I have the audience participate by roaring for the tiger. I asked a group of fourth-graders what this story taught them, and they told me such things as:

Don't trust wild animals.
Pray when you are in trouble.
Don't panic, help will come.
Do what your parents tell you to do.

The Swallow Queen's Gift

Many years ago, in old Korea, an old man was about to die, so he called his sons—Nolbu and Hungbu—and their families to his bedside.

"It is time to burn my rice bowl and chopsticks. I will be joining my ancestors soon," the old man wheezed.

"No, honorable Father, " the sons protested, "drink this broth, and you will feel strong again."

"I cannot live forever. It is time for me to rest. But before I go I want you to promise me that you will take care of the plants and trees and animals on our land."

"Yes, most honored Father, we will," the two brothers replied in earnest.

"Promise me that you will treat anyone who steps onto our property as a relative and friend. This is the best way to establish good relations with our neighbors."

"Yes, we promise."

"Most important of all I want you to promise me one more thing so that I can die in peace."

"Yes! Anything you say," they all replied.

"Take good care of one another. Do not fight or quarrel. There is enough room in this house for both families and enough food for all. Promise me this so that I can die in peace."

Both families vowed to their father and to one another with all their hearts that they would live harmoniously together. Later that night, the old man passed away and joined his ancestors. Both families mourned for they missed him already.

After the first year of mourning, selfishness and greed began to set in. Nolbu's wife made Hungbu's wife and children do all the housework while she and her children played and made messes that Hungbu's children had to clean up. In Korea the younger brother and spouse must serve the older brother and spouse, which Hungbu and his wife did faithfully. Nolbu's wife made Hungbu's wife and children cook for them, but they were not allowed to eat at the table with them.

"If you are hungry, you must eat the scraps from our plates after we are through. If that is not enough, go in the garbage and eat!" Nolbu's wife ordered.

Nolbu started to think how well off his family could live if he kicked Hungbu and his family out and kept the house, land, and money he had inherited for his own family. Even though Hungbu and his family never quarreled with Nolbu's family, Nolbu announced one day that Hungbu must move out.

"Hungbu, now that my wife is with child again there will not be enough room for both our families. I want you to take your wife and children and move out."

"But, older brother, where shall we live?"

"I don't care. You must move out this day!"

Hungbu and his family were thrown out with only the clothes on their backs. They were scared that they would die in the cold and rain. They did not know what would become of them, but Hungbu told his family: "If we all work together, we can survive. Each one of us must have a job to do."

Soon they came upon a small hut that they patched up. It was so small that when Hungbu lay down inside, his feet stuck outside the door. That night when the children were asleep, his wife complained, "Husband, what will we do in the winter? The snow and ice will come through the cracks, and we will freeze to death." But Hungbu could only think of good things. Holding her by the hand he replied: "Look! Through the cracks in the roof we can see the twinkling stars, and the moon is shining its beam on your face. You look so radiant."

She had to admit that it was beautiful. "But, husband, what will we do in the winter for food? We will starve to death."

"No, wife, we can hunt and fish and plant a garden. We can store up enough food for the winter. If you and I and the children work together as a team, we can survive."

That is exactly what they did, and somehow they managed to survive the winter. One spring day Hungbu stepped out of their hut and found that a mother and father swallow had built a nest in the eave of their house.

"This is a good sign that they have decided to live among us. Swallows are a sign of good fortune. Let us be careful not to scare them or bump the nest," Hungbu admonished.

Soon the babies hatched out of the eggs and were chirping constantly for food. One of the babies decided he wanted to fly, so he perched himself on the edge of the nest and took a leap. CRASH! He fell to the ground. Hungbu carefully picked up the baby: "Do not be afraid. Let me help you." Hungbu tied the bird's leg with a cloth, and the children brought water and sesame seeds. The bird grew and grew until one day it was able to fly to the warm, southern regions for the winter.

That young swallow told the Swallow Queen: "Hungbu and his family were so nice to me. They gave me seeds to eat, water to drink, and a place to sleep 'til I grew strong. Look, now I can fly."

"Yes," she answered, "let us reward him. Give him this seed." In the spring when the flowers started to bloom, the swallow put the seed in his beak, flew over, and dropped the seed in front of Hungbu.

"Thank you, Swallow. Children! Wife! Let us plant this seed together and see what grows. It looks like a gourd seed."

Soon after they planted it, the seed sprouted and began to grow huge, green leaves. A few weeks later there were three yellow blossoms growing, and they turned into large gourds.

"Let's open them up and see what is inside!" the children exclaimed. So they borrowed a big, long saw—the kind that needs a person on each end to push and pull. The mother and son pushed on one end as the father and daughter pulled on the other. When the gourd fell open, they all exclaimed together: "Rice! Tons of rice!"

"We have enough rice to last us the rest of our lives!" The wife was overjoyed. They cupped their hands and scooped up rice and let it fall through their fingers.

"Cool, heavy rice. It feels so good," Hungbu marveled.

"Let's open up the second gourd!" the children urged. They sawed, pushing and pulling. When the second opened up, yards and yards of silk material in many colors slipped out.

"Red, green, yellow, pink, blue with gold and silver painted on it!" the wife commented in wonder again. "We have enough material for clothes for the rest of our lives."

"We have one more gourd to open. I wonder what could be in this one."

As the third gourd was about to open, the daughter caught a glimpse and reported, "I see something glittering and shiny." Then many jewels and gems tumbled out.

"Gold!"

"Silver!"

"Pearls! We have enough wealth to buy anything we want for the rest of our lives!" Hungbu shouted.

"Let us build a house with 100 rooms!" Hungbu's wife proposed.

Now Hungbu's family was happy! They had everything they needed and more. One day, as Hungbu and his family were making themselves comfortable in their new home, Nolbu happened to look outside his house and see a huge mansion that he had not noticed before. He decided to take a closer look. As he neared the mansion, it appeared bigger and bigger. To his great surprise there was his brother, Hungbu, and his family living there. They wore beautiful clothes and jewelry and ate expensive delicacies.

"How did you get so rich so fast?" he demanded.

Hungbu replied: "We took care of a baby swallow that hurt itself, and the very next spring it flew by and dropped a gourd seed. We planted it and took care of it together—all of us. Three gourds grew, and out of the gourds came all these riches. Please, older brother, come live with us. There is more than enough for both of our families."

"No," Nolbu replied, "I will find my own fortune." Nolbu set out to find a bird. "Here birdie, birdie," he called. Finally he found one hiding in the trunk of a tree. He threw it on the ground so that it would be injured. "Let me fix you up," he said as he roughly tied its leg up with a cloth. "Now fly away, and bring me back a seed, and make me richer than my brother." Nolbu threw the bird in the air, but it fell to the ground and limped away. The other birds had to carry it south for the winter. When it reached the Swallow Queen, he cried in pain: "Nolbu was so mean to me! He hurt me. I cannot fly."

"Yes, we shall fix him. Give him this seed." It looked just like the other seed. In the spring when the swallow was mended enough, it took the seed in its beak and dropped it in front of Nolbu.

"At last I shall be rich, rich, rich!"

Nolbu planted the seed, and it grew just as fast as Hungbu's seed. Two yellow blossoms grew and out of the blossoms grew two large gourds.

"This is not fair. My brother got three, and I only get two. I will have to do it again and again until I get more than he."

His wife and children came out to take a look and demanded to open them. They sawed open the first gourd.

"EEEEEKK!! Spiders!"

"Scorpions!"

"Snakes!" They all ran to hide.

"This second gourd must have jewels in it. Come help me open it," Nolbu ordered.

Upon opening the second gourd a big flood of water and wind rushed out and swept away their home and land. Now Nolbu's family was wet, cold, and scared. All they could think to do was to go to Hungbu and ask for forgiveness.

"Hungbu, we are sorry for the way we treated you and your family. May we live with you for our home has washed away. We promise to treat you fairly."

"I am sorry for what has happened to you. Yes, older brother, please come live with us. This is the way our father wanted us to live."

From that day on, the two families lived in harmony.

Storyteller's Notes

When I tell this story to young audiences, I have them pair up and act out sawing open the gourds. Then on the count of three, all help open them up. For Hungbu's gourd with jewels I throw out plastic rings and necklaces. For the gourd with the bugs, I throw plastic spiders, snakes, and scorpions into the audience.

Many people tell me this story reminds them of "Jack and the Bean-stalk." At first I thought the magic seed was a trivial commonality, but then I realized that the magic seed was the turning point of both the stories. When the seed sprouts, it grows gourds and rewards Hungbu in one way but grows and rewards Jack in another because of cultural differences.

The Magic Vase

A very long time ago there lived a kind, gentle fisherman who had the ill fortune of being married to a cruel and greedy woman. One snowy, winter day he looked out to the sea and shook his head.

"This is not a good day for fishing. I shall mend some nets," he muttered to himself.

His wife overheard him and scolded: "You had better get out there this instant. We have barely enough fish to last us the week."

"The fish will not bite on a day like today. I would be wasting my time. My time is better spent mending nets and working around the house," the fisherman replied.

"You are making excuses to be lazy. I want a new dress to show off to our neighbors. So get out there, and don't return 'til you have caught some sizable fish to sell!" she demanded.

"As you wish," the fisherman replied for he knew she would give him no peace, and the thought of her nagging him was worse than being out in the storm.

He struggled and struggled to throw his net into the water and pull it out against the raging wind and high waves. Again and again he threw his net into the water and pulled it out though all he caught was seaweed, which he had to remove. Just when he thought the crashing waves were going to capsize his boat, he felt something heavy in his net. He was disappointed to find that it was only an old vase. He started to throw it back, but for some odd reason decided to keep it.

After a few more futile attempts to catch fish, the fisherman left his boat on the beach and walked home carrying the vase under his arm.

"Are you carrying fish in that dirty old vase?" his wife asked as soon as she saw him.

"No, this is all I caught," he replied. "I didn't pull in a single fish. I told you it was useless."

"You should have thrown back that dirty old vase!" she yelled at him.

"I thought we could clean it up and use it. It really isn't bad looking," he answered and went into the house.

"I do not want that ugly thing in my house!" she shrieked and grabbed it out of his hands and was ready to throw it out.

"Please let me wash it up and . . . "

"Poof!" Out came a noise from the vase, and the room filled with thick smoke. Then a young man appeared within the smoke. The husband and wife were speechless and a little fearful.

"Do not be afraid," spoke the young man standing before them. "I am here to grant you any wish you desire. Just rub the vase three times, and say what it is your heart desires. But choose well, for I can grant you only three wishes."

Then with a "Poof!" the young man and smoke appeared to be sucked back into the vase.

"Husband, for once you did something right!" the wife exclaimed. "Rice! Let's ask for rice!"

"Yes, yes. Let's ask for rice," agreed the fisherman, and he rubbed the vase three times asking for rice. At that very instant a gigantic mountain of rice filled the entire yard.

The fisherman and his wife danced for joy until they fell on the rice exhausted. A few minutes later the wife grabbed the vase and rubbed it.

"Poof!" the young man appeared in a cloud of smoke.

Smiling with delight the woman ordered, "Make us the richest people in this town."

"Go inside your house and take a look," spoke the young man, and he disappeared into the vase as before.

When the woman ran into the house, she screamed with ecstacy for gold and silver coins and all kinds of jewelry of precious gems were piled on the floor. She tossed the coins and jewelry up in the air. "What a wonderful vase! It is so wonderful!"

An hour later the woman turned to her husband and said, "Go back to the ocean and find another vase like this one."

"What?" cried the fisherman. "You've got all this wealth, and you want more? You are too greedy."

"We only have one more wish with this vase, and I have so many more things I want. Don't come home 'til you find another vase!" she ordered.

The poor fisherman left shaking his head and disgusted. The woman sat in front of a mirror to admire herself with all the jewelry draped about her. Suddenly she threw the mirror on the floor and screamed, "Why am I so ugly?" Then she had an idea. She grabbed the vase and rubbed it three times.

"Poof!" The young man appeared. "What is your wish?"

"Make me beautiful," ordered the woman.

The young man spoke not a word but nodded his head then disappeared into the vase as before.

The woman grabbed another mirror and looked at herself. "I am so beautiful and young." Immediately she frowned. "Now that I am so young and beautiful, I cannot live with that old, ugly husband of mine. When he comes back with another vase, I will have to wish him away."

She took the vase and was ready to throw it out when, "Poof!" the young man appeared for a fourth time. "Since you have wished a fourth wish, all the previous wishes are undone."

When the woman looked into the mirror, her reflection was that of the old, ugly face again. She screamed in terror and dropped the mirror, and it shattered into hundreds of pieces. Instantly a great wind swirled and blew away all the coins, jewels, the house, and the greedy woman.

Out on the ocean, the fisherman sat in his tossing boat and saw his wife and house blow away. Then he saw a large turtle that swam around and around his boat, beckoning him to get on its back. When the fisherman finally got on its back, it dove down into the water and carried him to the bottom of the sea.

The Dragon King invited the fisherman to live with him in his palace and gave him a loving and kind wife. There they all lived a long, happy, and harmonious life.

Photo from Korean Cultural Center.

Storyteller's Notes

How delightful to find a story of the proverbial genie in a magic vase that grants three wishes! Yet one must be careful what one wishes because it is more important what is inside the person than the outer trappings. As Jesus said: "Seek ye first the kingdom of Heaven and righteousness, and all the rest will be added unto you."

Who Shall Marry Rat's Daughter?

Mr. and Mrs. Rat only had one child, a daughter. As you can imagine, they doted on her from dawn 'til dusk. They wanted only the best for her, especially when it came time to choose a husband for her. They named off all the eligible rats they knew, but decided that none of them was good enough for their precious daughter.

Then one day Mr. Rat announced to his wife, "I know who will make the perfect husband for our sweet little darling: Mr. Sun."

"Why do you think Mr. Sun will be the perfect husband for her?" asked Mrs. Rat.

"Because he is the most powerful force in the world," answered Mr. Rat.

"You are right!" exclaimed Mrs. Rat. "He is magnificent. Let us ask him immediately."

The couple went out into their garden where the sun was shining down. "Mr. Sun! Oh, Mr. Sun!" they called as loudly as they could.

"Yes, what can I do for you?" replied the sun.

"My wife and I would like to offer our daughter's hand in marriage," Mr. Rat stated proudly.

"I am quite honored," said the sun, "but why do you want me to marry her?"

"Because you are most magnificent, and there is no other as powerful as you in the world," Mr. Rat answered. Mrs. Rat nodded in agreement.

"I am delighted that you think so highly of me," said Mr. Sun, "but you must know that there is one more powerful than I."

"Who could that be?" asked the surprised Mr. Rat.

"Mr. Cloud. I am powerless when he floats by and covers me up."

"Yes, yes. Rightly so, rightly so," said Mr. Rat, nodding to himself. "Come, come, my dear," he said as he took Mrs. Rat by the hand. "We must see Mr. Cloud."

The two climbed a nearby mountain over which a gigantic, billowy cloud hung. They called to Mr. Cloud and told him what they had heard from Mr. Sun and offered him their daughter in marriage.

But Mr. Cloud responded: "What Mr. Sun told you is correct. However, I have no power when I meet Mr. Wind. Wherever he blows, I must go."

"Yes, of course! Yes, of course!" exclaimed Mr. and Mrs. Rat as they went down the mountain to find Mr. Wind.

They found Mr. Wind in a grove of pine trees. "I am strong," he acknowledged upon hearing their story. "I can blow down a house, topple over trees, and even churn up the ocean. But however I try, I cannot budge a stone Buddha."

"Then we will have to ask a stone Buddha," resolved Mr. Rat, and the couple hurried off further down the trail to the biggest stone Buddha they knew.

"I am flattered that you want me to marry your daughter," said Mr. Stone Buddha, "but I don't think I am right for your daughter either. I am not the strongest in the world. There is someone who can make me fall over easily."

"Please, Mr. Stone Buddha, tell us who," begged Mr. Rat.

"It is none other than you and your mole cousins. Your race is incredibly strong. Every day I live in fear that one of you will burrow under my feet, and I will topple right over. I am no match for you."

"Thank you. You have been most helpful," said Mr. Rat with new realization.

And so it was and always has been that the rats' daughters always marry rats.

Star-Crossed Lovers

In the Kingdom of the South lived a king whose first wife was barren and died of an illness in her thirties. It was not until he remarried that he at last had a child, and he treasured his daughter above all. Her birth was celebrated for 100 days.

The princess grew to be both graceful and beautiful. Many suitors flocked to the palace to win her heart. On her eighteenth birthday the king pronounced, "It is time you should be married."

His daughter answered cajolingly, "Your Majesty, I am still only a child and too young to be married." The king conceded, thinking she was afraid to leave his protection.

The truth was, she desperately wanted to marry. For five years she had been in love with a young prince from the Northern Kingdom who had visited her on her birthday and given her a gift. The prince and princess had been enchanted with each other, but a few years afterward the kings of the North and South had a quarrel and became enemies. It was impossible for the children to declare their love publicly, and marriage was out of the question.

Two years passed, and the king could not wait any longer, so he arranged a marriage for his daughter. The princess, knowing she could not stall any longer, left the palace in the middle of the night to find her first love, the prince of the North.

Leaving the castle, the princess journeyed on foot, climbing hills and crossing rivers. When darkness fell, she realized how alone and frightened she was. But she spoke to herself, "I must be strong so that I can find my prince. There is no other life for me." She knelt on the ground and prayed with all her soul that she would find him. As she was praying, she fell asleep and dreamed of the handsome prince.

When the princess awoke, the sun had risen, so she continued on her difficult journey, eating wild berries and nuts along the way. She came to a small pond that she knelt at to take a drink, and when she looked into the water, she was horrified at her own reflection. Her face was dirty, and her hair was a tangled mess. She bathed herself and did her best to restore her appearance.

Along the way the princess met a kind-looking old woman carrying a basket.

"Is the North Kingdom far from here?" the princess asked.

"The North Kingdom! Gracious, you are going very far!" the old woman replied. "Let me show you the way." Then she gave the princess some food from her basket to give her extra nourishment for the journey. The old woman led her to the top of a hill and pointed out the way to the North Kingdom. When the princess realized that she must cross the cold, blue sea, her heart sank. She carefully walked down to the seashore, sat down, and started to weep.

A flock of birds that had been watching sympathetically flew to the princess.

"Do not weep. We will carry you over the sea if you weave a net of the tall grass."

All night long the princess wove by the firelight. In the morning she enveloped herself in the net, and the birds took that net in their beaks and flew her across the waters.

It was evening when the princess arrived at the palace of the North. When she was granted permission to speak with the king, she spoke to him of her love for his son and all that she had given up for him. The king was moved by her story but could not allow them to marry because of the enmity between the two kingdoms. He did not even allow his son to see the princess before he turned her out.

With great sadness the princess returned to the shore from whence she had come. The waves glimmered in the moonlight and seemed so inviting. With one last thought of the prince she loved, she threw herself into the sea. She was discovered the next day by fishermen, her lifeless body washed up ashore.

When the prince heard all that the princess of the South had done for him out of love, he was devastated beyond measure. He had fallen in love with her since the day they met and knew there was no other for him. His heart broken forever, he flung himself into the sea to join his beloved princess in the next life.

The king of the North grieved bitterly over the loss of his only son. He so regretted his harsh actions that resulted in the death of the princess and his son that he went to reconcile his differences with the king of the South Kingdom. When the two kings finally resolved their enmity, they prayed together that the prince and princess would be reborn as flowering trees as a sign of forgiveness.

On the prince's grave a tree with crimson flowers emerged and leaned toward the South. On the princess' grave a tree with pure white flowers blossomed leaning toward the North. The two trees containing the spirits of the princess and prince still grow toward each other, stretching in silent longing for one another.

Storyteller's Notes

This story reminds me so much of Shakespeare's "Romeo and Juliet." This is what excites me about researching folktales from many cultures: They all have some of the same themes. As the saying goes, "Great minds think alike." Human nature is truly similar the world over.

Photographs and Artwork

Photographs courtesy of Korean Cultural Center unless otherwise noted.

Above: Korean see-saw (nŏlttwigi). The Korean women in ancient times were never allowed out of the fenced courtyard. They devised this game of see-saw to be able to see over the fence. The same is true for the tall swings; they swing high enough to see over the fence.

Korean hacky-sack (chegi ch'agi)

Deer and symbols of long life.

Playful tiger cubs.

Lotus Lantern Avalokitesvara of the Sea. Avalokitesvara is the Bodhisattva of Perfect Compassion and was born out of the ray of light from the eye of Buddha Amitabha. The sea represents the Sea of Suffering. The lotus lantern represents the light of wisdom and enlightenment within each of us. Buddha's last words were "Be a lamp unto thyself."
Art by Brian Barry.

Chijang Bosal Taengwha. Bosal is a selfless being of compassion. *Taengwha* is the Korean word for temple painting. Chijang vowed to rescue all sentient beings from suffering before entering Nirvana himself and is often referred to as the "Bodhisattva of Hells."

Dragon and deer paintings.

Taking a prisoner to jail.

Portrait of a Korean scholar.

Kim Hongdo
Korean wrestling.

Farmer's music (nongak).

Colorful Korean chest from the Chosŏn period.

Jewels of the Buddhas
and Bodhisattvas,
symbols of their
compassionate
teachings and deeds.
Art by Brian Barry.

Bodhidharma brought meditation to
China in the fourth century and sat
in front of a blank wall for nine years
in his quest to become enlightened.
Therefore, he is symbolic of a ferocious
determination to become enlightened
through meditation. He is considered
the father of Zen meditation in the
East.
Art by Brian Barry.

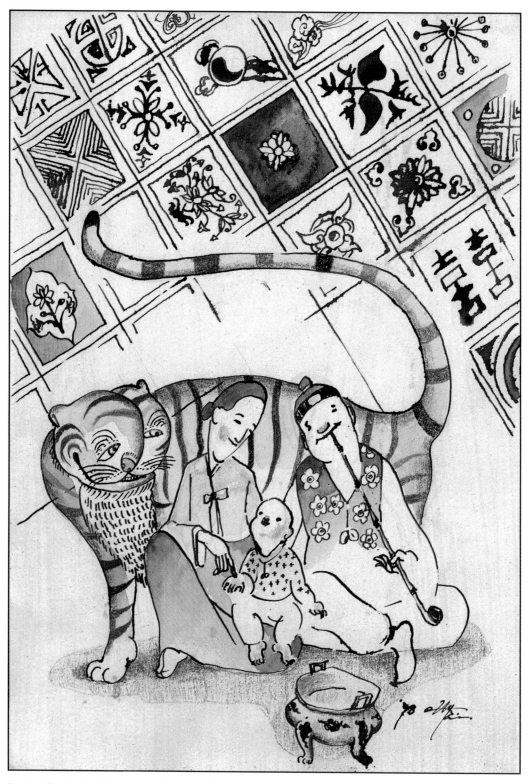

Painting by Kim Eui Kyoo, Ansan City, South Korea.

Section III

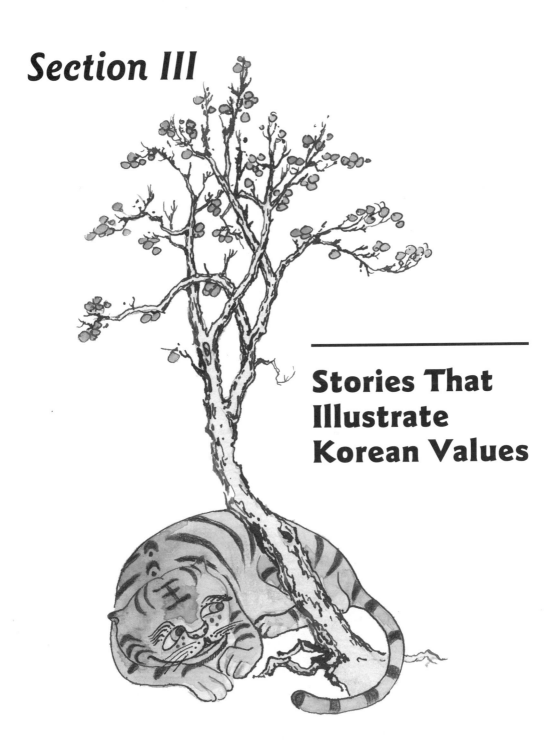

Stories That Illustrate Korean Values

Yun Ok's Potion

Yun Ok was very upset. Every day she was becoming more depressed. You see, her husband had gone off to war for three years, and for three long years she had not seen him. When he came back, he was a different man than when he had left. For instance, before he left he used to like her cooking and thank her for the wonderful meals that she cooked, but since he came back he took one bite of food and pushed it aside. "Yuck!" Before he went to war, they had long conversations into the night, but now he did not want to talk with anybody. He would just go into his dark room and stare. Yun Ok didn't know what she was to do. Then she thought of the wise mountain sage, perhaps he could help her. Maybe he would make a magic potion to change him back into the man he used to be. She climbed up the hill where the sage lived and knocked on the door.

"Come in," he ordered. "What do you want?"

"Most venerated one," she bowed deeply, "my husband has come back from fighting in the war, but since he came back he does not eat or sleep or want to talk."

"Such is common when men go to war. They see horrible, frightening things. Go on with your story," he answered,

"There isn't anymore to my story. That's it. He is miserable and making me miserable. Can you make a magic potion to change him back into the man he used to be?" Yun Ok petitioned.

"Potions, potions! Do you think there is a magic potion to solve everything in the world?" scowled the sage.

"Please, you must help me. I'm afraid he will get sick and die. I still love him very much."

"I will see what I can do. Come back in three days, and I will have an answer for you," the sage replied with a change in his voice.

Yun Ok walked home very hopeful. When she arrived home, her husband yelled at her: "Where have you been? Where is my dinner?" She fixed him some food, but he pushed it away and went to his room. She was not so upset because she told herself, "Only three more days, and he will be all right."

When three days had passed, she climbed the hill and knocked on the door of the wise mountain sage.

"Come in," he beckoned her.

She bowed respectfully to him. "I have the potion, but the most essential ingredient in this magic potion is the whisker of a living tiger. You must bring it to me."

"How can I do that? No one even goes near the mountain where the tiger lives. The tiger is more ferocious than my husband!"

"If it is important to you, you will find a way." He turned his back, not wanting to speak anymore. Yun Ok was very disappointed and discouraged. She thought he was going to answer her problem, instead he gave her another problem.

When she arrived home, her husband yelled at her: "Where have you been. Where is my dinner?" She fixed him some food, but he pushed it away. She was miserable and decided she had to do something. So she took that bowl of food that her husband did not eat and took it to the mountain where the

tiger lived. She set the bowl down at the base of the mountain then called to the tiger. "Come eat. I fixed you a good meal." The tiger came out and roared at her. She ran down the mountain as fast as she could. She was so scared!

When she arrived home, her husband yelled at her.

"I get roared at by my husband and roared at by the tiger. I can't stand this. I have to do something." So the next week she fixed a bigger bowl of food and took it further up the mountain. She set the bowl down on the ground and called to the tiger. "Come and eat. I fixed you a very special meal with spicy gravy." But the tiger came out and roared at her. She ran down the mountain as fast as she could with her heart pounding away. "This will never work. I will never go up there again."

But when she returned home, her husband yelled at her. "I must try one more time. If that doesn't work, I don't know what I will do."

The next week she carried a gigantic bowl of food higher and higher up the mountain. It was very heavy and hard to carry, but she placed it at the opening of the cave of the tiger. As she set the bowl down, she looked into the dark cave and saw the yellow eyes of the tiger glowing out at her. Her heart pounded, but she stayed. And to her surprise he came out and ate right in front of her.

She stroked the tiger and said: "I will not hurt you. I just want one whisker for the magic potion. Please, may I have one whisker?" She took out a pair of clippers and snipped one whisker and held it tightly. "Thank-you, tiger, thank you." Then she backed away, not wanting to frighten the tiger, and ran down the mountain to the home of the wise mountain sage.

"I have it. I have the tiger's whisker!"

The sage took the whisker and examined it, turning it around and around, "Yes, indeed, it is the whisker of a living tiger." Then he threw it into the fire, and it burned up.

Now, Yun Ok had never yelled at a man before, because in Korea, a woman yelling at her husband could be grounds for divorce. Yet she yelled at the sage now. "That was for the magic potion! You said. Now all my work is for nothing!" she cried.

"Yun Ok, please calm down. The whisker is not needed anymore. Tell me how you got the whisker."

Yun Ok sat down and told him. "Every day I prepared a bowl of food for the tiger and called to him in a calm tone of voice. I told him I would not hurt him. Then today to my surprise he came right out of his cave and ate."

"Yes, you tamed the tiger with your patience and understanding. That took a lot of courage. Now go home and do the same with your husband."

All the way home Yun Ok thought over and over in her mind this lesson that she learned from the wise mountain sage.

Storyteller's Notes

When I tell this story, many times I signal to my young audience when I want them to roar for the tiger. In this way the audience participates in the story, and the storyteller does not wear out his or her voice. Also when I tell this story, I like to play on the harp and sing the following song.

Arirang
Paraphrased by Lindy Soon Curry

Arirang, arirang, arariyo.
Over the Arirang Hill you must go.
How I wish you would not go away.
It is very far and I want you to stay.
Arirang, arirang, arariyo.
Over the Arirang Hill you must go.
Many stars twinkle in the heaven above,
Yet my heart is saddened because you are leaving me.
Arirang, arirang, arariyo.
Over the Arirang Hill you must go.
Is there a spell on Arirang Hill?
The further I climb the taller it appears.

This is the most popular of all Korean folk songs. The song took its name from Arirang Hill, a small hill in the northeastern outskirts of Seoul leading to one of the public cemeteries. Since Korea is a mountainous country, each province has its own Arirang Hill.

This is the very first Korean story I was able to tell because it was my favorite Korean story. I was impressed with the idea of taming a tiger. I, being very petite, have had to deal with many physical fears and challenges. How was I going to be able to drive a car? What kind of career would best suit me? What group of people should I identify with? Just the challenge of telling a story in front of audiences was a fear to overcome, but with each telling I became more adept.

Life has a way of treating us the way the sage treated Yun Ok—it puts us through hardships and challenges then appears to change the rules. However, what one learns from previous experiences helps one to overcome the next challenge, and life gets easier and less scary. This is a story of enduring love, courage, patience. Think of the husband, wife, tiger, and sage as all parts of yourself. We all have parts of us that are scared, beastly, and wise. We have it within us to overcome our fears.

The Value of Salt

When the son of an aristocratic man fell in love with the daughter of a salt peddler, the parents were against it because in those days society was rigidly segregated into classes according to occupation, and peddling salt was one of the lowest.

Much to his parents' embarrassment, the young man refused all other marriage proposals, saying he would not marry at all if he could not marry the daughter of the salt peddler. Eventually, his parents consented, and the two were married.

However, the in-laws made life miserable for the girl. Despite her husband's protests, they verbally abused her and ridiculed her looks. The girl cried in secret but did not even complain to her husband. She performed her daily chores faithfully.

You can imagine how upset her parents were to learn of how their sweet, dutiful daughter was treated.

"I wish we could do something to make life better for her. I can't eat or sleep thinking how horrible it must be to live in a household where everyone looks down on you," sighed the salt peddler.

"I have an idea," the wife spoke up after some thought. "Let's invite her parents-in-law to dinner."

"I don't think they will come," cautioned the salt peddler.

"If we insist, they must, at least this once. And this is what I plan to do . . . " she explained.

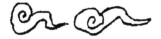

The salt peddler agreed that it was a good plan. Just as they expected, the in-laws laughed and refused the dinner invitation, but the salt peddler, his wife, and their own son were so insistent that they finally agreed.

The salt peddler and his wife humbly welcomed the in-laws into their home. As was the custom, the salt peddler and the father-in-law sat down to drink wine. After the wine, the father-in-law ate one of the delicacies the wife had prepared. He could not believe how strange it tasted. It was so bland that he wanted to spit it out and could not take another bite.

The wife placed a table of food in front of the mother-in-law. The mother-in-law ate some rice and then a morsel of a side dish. It was very bland. She drank a spoonful of soup that was also tasteless. Finally, she put down her chopsticks, indicating she was finished eating.

"Please eat some more," said the salt peddler's wife. "You must be hungry after your journey."

"No, thank you. I can't for I am still full from breakfast," lied the mother-in-law.

"Have another drink," said the salt peddler, handing another wine cup to the father-in-law.

"Oh, no, no," replied the father-in-law. "I can't eat another bite, so there's no way I can drink."

"Then there is something I must say," spoke the salt peddler. "I know you are not eating because the food has no taste. It is tasteless because it has not a single grain of salt. I instructed my wife to make it that way to show you how indispensable salt is to our diet. As you have just experienced, it is impossible to eat without it. Everyone from the king to beggars must have salt. Wealthy people like you must have salt to make food palatable. And there must be someone to make it available for them. Just as there must be farmers, merchants, butchers, and rulers. What kind of world would it be without them? I may be speaking out of turn, but I wanted to explain to you the value of salt and ask you to love my daughter."

The parents-in-law stood up and low bowed to the salt peddler and his wife. "You are entirely correct. No matter how wealthy a person is, he cannot live without salt," acknowledged the father-in-law with a humble voice. "Thank you for demonstrating to me that we all need one another to survive in this world."

From that day on, the wealthy family and the salt peddler's family spent many enjoyable visits together. Moreover, the wealthy couple loved their daughter-in-law and had only words of praise for her.

The Good Neighbor

It was an extremely hot, muggy summer day in the southern part of Korea. Everyone was seeking shade, including a young man who finally spotted a large zelkova tree across the street. When he arrived, he was surprised to see a well-dressed old man asleep on a rush mat under the tree. Not wanting to disturb him, the young man sat down very quietly to rest in the shade with his back against the tree and was soon snoozing.

He was rudely awakened by the old man: "You rascal, you are sitting in my shade!"

"Excuse me? What did you say?"

"I said, 'Get out of my shade.' "

"This tree belongs to all the town. How can you say this is your shade?"

"My grandfather's grandfather planted this tree. That makes it mine. Now get out immediately."

"Very well," the young man replied politely. Then he asked in a more serious tone, "If this is your shade, would you mind selling it to me?" He pulled out some coins.

"Of course," the old man chuckled, "give me five *nyang*, and it is yours."

The young man gave the old man five *nyang* (Korean coins) and lay down in the shade. The old man snickered to himself and thought what a fool the young man was to buy the shade of a tree. Then he moved his rush mat to another shade tree.

As the sun moved across the sky, the shadow of the tree grew longer and extended into the old man's yard. The young man followed the tree's shadow and sat down in the yard.

"What are you doing sitting in another man's yard!" screamed the old man. "Get out of my yard!"

"What is wrong, sir? I am only sitting in the shade you sold me."

"You are trespassing. Get out!"

"You are the one trespassing since I own the shade. You are standing in my shade."

Fussing and fuming the old man stomped into his house. Soon the shade extended onto the porch, so the young man got up and moved onto the porch. A while later the young man got up and opened the door and walked right in and sat on a pillow on the floor.

"Get out, you impudent fool! You cannot walk into a man's house without permission!"

"The shadow of the tree which you sold me is over this house. Therefore, I have every right to be here."

"You do not. I shall call the police to throw you out and into jail."

"What will you tell them? That you sold me the shade and that I am sitting in the shade?"

"I will give you back your five *nyang* if you will give me back my house."

"I would not think of giving up this nice shade."

It did not take long for people of the village to get word of this incident, and people laughed at the old man as they passed him, calling him the "greedy old shade seller" and saying, "Will you sell me some shade?"

The old man got so disgusted that he finally packed some of his belongings and moved his family out of town. This left the young man with not only the shade of the tree but a house and land as well. Being a generous soul, he shared the house, land, and shade with all the villagers and became known as "the good neighbor."

Storyteller's Notes

This tall tale I use to illustrate how neighbors should treat one another and how generosity wins over stinginess.

I like to sing the following Korean folk song to introduce and conclude this story because I feel that the story could have been told by the willow tree who observed all. I especially delight in the line "No need for bitterness" because it is best to make peace with what happens in one's life.

Hung Taryong
Paraphrased by Lindy Soon Curry

Weeping willow tree, Hung! Hung!
Leaning over Samkori, Hung! Hung!
You have witnessed so much bliss,
Standing so tranquilly, Hung! Hung!
E he ya e he ya e he ya,
No need for bitterness, Hung! Hung!
Life progresses rapidly, Hung! Hung!
Time, slow your racing, Hung! Hung!
My youthful days are gone,
For my hair turns very grey, Hung! Hung!
E he ya, e he ya, e he ya,
No need for bitterness, Hung! Hung!

The Honey Pot

There was once a very strict teacher of a small private school in a mountain village. As the students were busy working on their assignments, he would stealthily eat something from some kind of jar he kept behind his desk. The students from time to time observed this odd behavior and finally one brave student asked him: "Teacher, what are you eating? It must be very good tasting."

"Not at all. It's medicine," the teacher replied.

"Are you sick?" inquired the boys with concern.

"No, don't worry. It's something to give me more energy and strength in my old age. You must not eat any because it is very strong and could kill you." He fooled all but one clever student.

Several days later the teacher informed the class that he had to go to a meeting but that the students should practice their lessons until he returned. After a few minutes that one clever boy opened the teacher's small chest behind the desk to see for himself what he was always eating.

"You're going to get us all in trouble!" one of the boys yelled.

"Teacher will whip you for that!" said another.

"Why should he beat me? He lied to us. That is worse than what I am doing," explained the clever boy, and he placed the jar on the teacher's desk for all to see. "Look. This is honey, not medicine." Then he dipped his fingers into the jar and licked them.

All the other boys hurried to get a taste of the honey. Soon it was all gone. Suddenly they fell silent, wondering what was to become of them.

"Don't worry. I have a plan. Do as I say," said the clever boy. The clever boy picked up the teacher's ink stone and dropped it on the floor. The other boys were aghast when it broke.

"Why did you do that? Now we're in worse trouble!" the boys all shouted.

"You will soon see why. Now, lie down on the floor. When you hear the teacher enter the door, moan and groan and clutch your stomach as if it aches. I will take care of the rest."

Presently they heard the teacher coming through the squeaky gate.

"My stomach hurts! I'm dying!" The boys all cried rolling around on the floor.

"What is the matter?" exclaimed the teacher as he entered the scene.

"Teacher, they're all dying," explained the clever boy. "Everyone was playing around instead of doing their work and accidentally knocked over your ink stone. It broke," he went on, showing it to him. "We all felt so guilty that we ate your medicine to kill ourselves. Now we are writhing in pain."

The teacher smiled sheepishly at the clever boy and realizing what he had done merely said: "All right. Everyone get up. It is time to practice our calligraphy."

The teacher never again lied to his students nor tried to eat secretly in their presence. As for the clever boy, he grew up to become a government official and became famous for his keen wisdom and judgment.

The Weeping Princess

Once upon a time in the ancient walled city of Pyongyang, which is now the capital of North Korea, there lived a king whose youngest daughter was known as the Weeping Princess. She was called this because she was very sensitive and cried about so many things that it seemed as if she were crying all the time.

It was crowded in the streets the day she and her mother were being carried in the palanquin to the Spring Pavilion. The bearers stopped, and the herald yelled, "You dog, out of the way!" The youngest princess peeked out and saw a beggar boy lying in the mud.

"Hey, Pabo* Ondal! Get out of the way!" the herald screamed, kicking the boy. The princess was too scared to protest, but tears of compassion flowed from her eyes.

Her sisters groaned, "She's crying again, our Weeping Princess." And her mother worried that no man would want a wife who cried all the time.

Wild stories were being spread about the beggar Pabo Ondal and how he lived among the animals in the mountains. The king even heard some of the stories.

On New Year's Day, the youngest princess came with her brothers and sisters to the Grand Palace. As she made her bow to her father, the king, she tripped and stumbled. Tears ran down her cheeks.

"Now, now! Why are you crying on the first day of the new year?" asked the king. But his daughter cried even more. "She is impossible! If she keeps crying like this for every little thing, we will have to marry her off to the beggar, Pabo Ondal!" he teased.

The queen was aghast and felt she would faint. "Do not say such words on the first day of the new year," she chastised him for that would set the tone for the whole year and be a bad omen.

Everyone in the court heard the king's joke, and from then on the Weeping Princess was teased constantly that she would be the wife of Pabo Ondal.

The princess hid in the palace library and consoled herself by reading her favorite poems and stories. This too she had to keep a secret for fear of ridicule.

When the princess was sixteen, the king announced that it was time for her to marry. "I have arranged a most wonderful match with the son of noble Ko."

The princess imagined her life as a noblewoman—running a household under a mother-in-law's directions, with all the frivolous parties and court gossip for entertainment. She would have no time to herself or her secret studies. She knew that life would be intolerable.

"Sir, I cannot accept," whispered the princess with downcast eyes.

"What do you mean?" shouted the king. "I have arranged a fine match. You should be grateful! You will obey me!" he rebuked.

The desperate princess replied, "Most honored Father, please forgive me, but before I wed the son of noble Ko, I would be the wife of Pabo Ondal!"

"The wife of Pabo Ondal! Do not talk such nonsense. You will be married as I ordered!"

"But most esteemed Father," she argued in a panic, "you even said on New Year's that you would marry me to Pabo Ondal."

The king was beside himself with rage by now and thundered, "Go then to Pabo Ondal, and do not set foot in this house again!" The king then banished her from the palace.

That night just before dawn the princess left the palace alone and on foot for the very first time in her life. She was dressed in the traditional bride *hanbok* and carried one small bundle with gold pieces, which were a parting gift from her mother, the queen.

The princess walked in the direction of Peony Peak, for that is where Pabo Ondal was said to live. At sundown she came upon a spot near a shabby straw-roofed hut and sat down crying with tears of exhaustion and fear. Then a raspy voice startled her.

"Why are you crying?"

"I have come to marry Ondal," the princess was barely able to whisper.

"Why do you mock me?" the voice retorted.

"If Ondal won't have me," she replied, "then I will have no place to go for I have been banished from my home."

A man with unkempt hair wearing rags stepped closer to her and wiped away her tears with a cloth then took her by the hand. The princess timidly followed Ondal as he gathered roots and hunted in the forest. Ondal watched as she hand stitched fine linen garments to replace his old, ragged clothing. Finally by the end of the summer, they became accustomed to each other.

During the long, dark winter evenings, the princess recited her favorite poems to Ondal. Then she taught him how to read and write. The princess was amazed at how quickly he learned. She was endeared to him when she saw how gentle and kind he was to the forest creatures.

"It is terrible how the village people ridicule you and call you ugly names. I want them to learn the truth about you," she announced one day.

"Pay no attention, my wife, for we are happy now," he tried to comfort her.

"I want you to take these two gold pieces and buy a horse. The horse may be weak and lame as long as it is of good breeding," she instructed.

"I will be scorned and beaten," Ondal protested.

"No, you won't, for they will not even recognize you. You are no longer Pabo Ondal the beggar, and I am no Weeping Princess."

The next day Ondal returned with a gangly and dirty horse. The princess and Ondal cared for the horse until it grew strong enough for the princess to give Ondal riding lessons.

One year later the princess spoke to Ondal. "Husband, on the third day of the third month, the king will hold the Festival of the Hunters. You are ready to join the hunt this year." Ondal at first was hesitant, but the princess did not rest until he agreed.

At the hunting festival a mysterious rider cloaked as a commoner amazed the noble huntsmen with crafty and fearless maneuvers. Before they could ask him his name he disappeared. Everyone who witnessed it could talk of nothing else. Then they speculated that such a talented nobleman would surely enter the Festival of Scholars on the Full Moon Night of the fifth month, then they could find out his true identity. When the princess heard of this poetry contest, she told Ondal that he must enter. He only agreed when she said she would accompany him and observe.

As they entered the capital, the sounds of drums, flutes, and gongs filled the air. Many masked dancers and farmers' bands and peddlers crowded the streets. When evening came, Ondal joined the scholars at the Lotus Pavilion. The noblemen protested when they saw him in commoner's clothing. "Peasants can neither read nor write."

Ondal silenced them by replying, "Then what do you have to fear?" When it was finally Ondal's turn, he prepared his ink. Then with firm strokes he brushed the characters of his poem. All the judges were in awe of the simplicity, swiftness, and strength of his poem. One of the judges declared Ondal the winner, then read aloud from the scroll for all to hear. When he was finished, everyone in the audience applauded, and the princess wiped a tear from her eye. The king clapped the loudest and called the winner before him to receive the prize.

"Are you the skilled huntsman from the hunting festival?" the king interrogated.

"Royal Highness, I am he," Ondal replied.

"How is it possible that you have mastered the royal arts?" the king pressed on.

"Most noble sir, all that I have learned I owe to my esteemed wife."

"Then bring her here, for I would like to see her at once!"

The princess made her way up to the Lotus Pavilion to her husband's side. She bowed before the king. "Royal Highness," she explained, "my husband used to be known by the name Pabo Ondal."

Everyone spoke to one another in amazement. "The banished princess has returned!" "The stranger is Pabo Ondal, and he has won the king's poetry contest!"

Finally the king spoke. "My daughter has returned, bringing me a son worthy of honor. You have won my favor. What do you ask of me?"

"Honored Father, we ask only to serve you" was her reply.

And that is how it was that Ondal's services to the king in the years that followed were numerous and wonderful, but his true happiness and fulfillment were his wife and children who waited for him at the base of Peony Peak.

Storyteller's Notes

Pabo means fool or idiot. Thus Ondal and the princess were much misunderstood. This is a lovely story of "finding a jewel in the mud." Both the princess and Ondal had to find their talents and be true to themselves.

Across the Silvery Stream

High, high in the heavens lived the star king and queen. They had a beautiful daughter whose passion was to weave, and so she was known by her subjects as Chingnyo, which means "weaving maid." Every day her father and mother would visit her to see her creations of flowers, birds, and animals woven with many lovely colored threads.

One day her father came to her weaving room and was surprised by what he discovered. "What is the meaning of this? This is not a flower but the face of a man."

"Please forgive me, Father. I do not know what has come over me, but lately I have been lonely."

"I know what is happening, my precious. You are coming to the age that you should be married. I will ask all the wise men who the perfect match for you would be."

All the wise men of the heavenly kingdom were consulted, and it was agreed that the perfect match for the princess Chingnyo would be prince Kyonwu, the cowherder. Both kingdoms were delighted with the match, and so it was that the marriage day came quickly. Just before they were married they were given some marital advice. The parents both admonished that they must not neglect their heavenly duties and must complete their work. If they remembered to work first then play after their daily tasks were completed, they would be happy all of their lives.

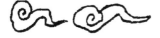

The first year they remembered this advice, but soon they were having so much fun together that they wanted to play all the time. The loom was becoming rusty and dusty from neglect. The constellations had no new clothes to wear and were freezing to death. The cows were wandering off and starving to death, and in turn the constellations were hungering also because the herd boy did not attend to them. When the star king was alerted to these conditions, he became extremely angry and called his daughter and son-in-law forth. They bowed to his throne and put their heads to the ground.

"Chingnyo, because you have neglected your duties, Kongjwi*, who has been mistreated by her stepmother and stepsister, has no clothes to wear to the banquet."

"I will start to weave her a dress immediately, most honorable father."

"I will see that you do. You and your lazy husband shall be separated forever. Chingnyo must stay on this side of the Silvery Stream (Milky Way), and Kyonwu must stay on the other!"

"Please do not do that, Father, for we will die of a broken heart!" Kyonwu begged. As the two newlyweds started to weep, the father took pity on them.

"Enough crying! I will let you see each other one day a year. On the seventh day of the seventh moon you may see each other for one day only!"

The two looked at each other with despair but had no choice but to obey. All year long as they wove and tended the cattle, respectively, they pined away for each other, hardly able to do their tasks. The year passed by painfully slowly. Finally on the seventh day of the seventh moon they rushed toward each other. They ran and they ran until they reach the Silvery Stream but could not cross.

"Chingnyo!"

"Kyonwu!" That is all they could do—call to each other from their side of the Silvery Stream.

"The Silvery Stream is too wide and deep to cross. What shall we do?" Chingnyo cried.

"Maybe we should ask the sun to help us!" Kyonwu cried back.

"No! Don't do that. If you do, it will be the next day, and we will have to wait a whole year to try again."

When they realized the futility of their plight, they sat down and cried copious tears that fell to the earth, causing a great monsoon and flood. All the animals of the forest were in a panic for they had never seen such rain. Their homes were being washed away, and some of the animals did not know how to swim.

Finally the animals went to the wise owl for advice. The owl told them the sad, sad story of the young newlyweds. The animals learned how the couple would not stop crying until they could cross the Silvery Stream and hold each other.

The nightingale sang out, "I can teach them my song so that they can sing to each other."

"That might help some, but that is not enough," the owl replied.

The crane spoke up, "I can teach them to dance, and that will make them feel better."

"No, that will not stop their crying," the owl insisted.

Finally the magpies and crows screeched, "We can fly up to the Silvery Stream and spread our wings to make a bridge so that they can walk across on our backs."

And so it is on the seventh day of the seventh moon that magpies and crows cannot be seen here on Earth for they are all up in the heavens making a bridge across the Silvery Stream. When the magpies and crows return the next day, there are feathers missing from their backs where Chingnyo and Kyonwu's feet stepped. And always the next day there is a little mist in the air as Chingnyo and Kyonwu weep just a little for they know they will see each other next year.

Astronomers all over the world have noted that the constellations Vega and Altair do come together on the seventh day of the seventh moon for a day and then part.

Storyteller's Notes

Koreans use the lunar calendar for most of their holidays, though recently they observe New Year's Day on January 1 and Christmas on December 25 as in the West. The Koreans have been preoccupied with the celestial bodies, and thus it affects Korean society. The weaving maiden is Vega, and herd boy is Altair. Astronomers note that they do come together once a year around the seven month between July and August.

*Kongjwi is the name of the Korean cinderella. (See "The Tale of Kongjwi.") It is Chingnyo who makes her a gown instead of the fairy god-mother as in the European versions.

Section IV

The Power of Stories

The Clever Wife

Pak Hongjip was born into a wealthy family. Since they had lots of leisure time, they were all expected to study and be learned men. But Hongjip refused to study. His father grew so frustrated with him that he threatened to disown him and throw him out into the streets like a common beggar.

One day Mr. Pak's brother came to visit, and this gave him an idea.

"Dear brother, will you do me a favor? Will you take Hongjip with you? I am so sick and tired of seeing this idiot. Even though he is fourteen, he still has not learned to read or write."

"Brother, no matter how dull he is, he is still your son. You can't disown him."

"If you do not take him, I will throw him out anyway."

Finally the brother agreed to take Hongjip with him and take care of him. The uncle was impressed by the nephew's handsome looks and thought him to be a congenial boy. The uncle resolved to win Hongjip over to study with kindness. Every day he sat down with his nephew and patiently worked with him. After many months, the boy had not learned a thing. His uncle finally realized what his brother was talking about.

"Why do you loathe studying so?" the uncle asked.

"Ever since I was a child, studying either gave me a headache or put me to sleep. But I do love to hear stories."

"What are we to do with you?" The uncle felt responsible for Hongjip since his father had disowned him. Hongjip was such a good-natured boy that he grew more and more fond of him.

A few years later Hongjip became a strong and handsome young man ready for marriage. The uncle was determined to arrange a marriage to a lovely bride from a good family for his nephew.

After making a few inquiries, he found out that the wealthy Mr. Kang had a beautiful daughter of marriageable age. He invited Mr. Kang over to his house for dinner to introduce his nephew to him.

"Mr. Kang, I hear you have a charming daughter, and I know of a young man who would be a good husband for her."

"That is kind of you, Mr. Pak, please tell me more about him."

"He is actually the son of my brother in Seoul."

"Really, not *the* Mr. Pak of Seoul!" Mr. Kang knew that the Paks were the one of the oldest and most respected families in Seoul and began wondering to himself why the Paks did not marry him to a better family. Was the boy blind, deaf, or sick?

The uncle sensed Mr. Kang's apprehension and summoned his nephew.

"Hongjip, this is Mr. Kang," his uncle introduced them.

"How do you do?" Hongjip bowed and replied in a strong, clear voice. Mr. Kang was impressed with Hongjip's appearance, but then asked: "Why do you want to marry him to my daughter? Our family is respectable but still beneath yours."

Hongjip's uncle explained that because the boy did not study, his father disowned him. This satisfied Mr. Kang, and he agreed to the marriage. Although Hongjip was uneducated, he was from an excellent family, and Mr. Kang had enough money to support his daughter and new son-in-law.

Hongjip and Mr. Kang's daughter were married and they lived happily except for the fact that Hongjip never read or studied.

"Why do you never read or study?" his wife asked.

"Please do not talk to me about studying, the mere mention of the word *study* causes my head to ache."

But his wife could not rest 'til she tried to teach him to read. Within a few months she too realized that he had not learned a thing. Finally she had an idea.

"What are you doing, husband?"

"Nothing."

"Then let us do something."

"What?"

"Let us teach each other some stories," she suggested.

"Good. I love stories."

So Hongjip's wife told her husband many stories, and he was mesmerized. He praised his wife for being such a good storyteller. When she finished, she asked him if he remembered any of the stories. Without hesitation, he recited all the stories word for word. His wife was amazed at his incredible memory. The next day she told him stories well into the night, and he memorized every one of them.

The next day Hongjip asked his wife, "Where do the stories come from?"

"From the books I read."

"Why do books give me such a headache when what is in them is so fascinating?"

"The more you read and study, the more interesting it becomes. And the more interesting it becomes, the easier it is to study."

"I had better start learning to study then."

Hongjip's wife taught her husband the basics of reading by using stories. Since Hongjip was actually very bright, he mastered the basics and was able to study by himself. Once he got into the habit of studying, he became quite engrossed in his studies. His wife gave him an insatiable thirst for learning, and within a few years he mastered the classics.

"Now I will teach you to write," his wife declared.

This too he tackled with great energy and soon surpassed many in his studies.

One day the king proclaimed an important public examination for scholars. Hongjip's wife urged him to take the examination.

"Husband, if you are publicly honored, your parents will receive you back once again as their son."

Hongjip went to Seoul and took the examination. When the results were announced, he was overjoyed that he achieved top honors. After the examination all the people went to his father, Mr. Pak, to congratulate him.

"Congratulations, Mr. Pak, on your son's award. Where did he receive his education?"

"All these years you have downplayed his intelligence. Is that how you motivated him to do so well?"

The old man was entirely in disbelief. Indeed, he had no clue as to what people were talking about.

Finally Hongjip went to his parents and explained how his wife had inspired him to learn to read and write by telling him stories. His father was elated.

"I must order a carriage to bring my daughter-in-law here for a celebration!"

And so a huge banquet and celebration was arranged to celebrate the return of his son as a respected member of the family.

Not long after his father took him back into the family, Hongjip became prime minister. But no matter how successful he became, he always gave his wife the credit for his success.

Storyteller's Notes

This story is an excellent illustration of how stories can be used as a learning tool! Educators are finally rediscovering how valuable stories are in teaching. Lawyers are also taking courses on storytelling to enhance their courtroom presentations, for they have found that the facts of the case are easier for jurors to remember in story form. Even if the events of the story did not happen, stories explain and illustrate truths. Moreover, stories paint pictures with words, and the resulting picture can motivate and inspire.

The Pouch of Stories

There was once a boy, the son of a wealthy family, who loved to have stories told to him. Every time this boy met someone new, he would beg them to tell him a new and different story. After hearing the stories, he stored them in a pouch that he tied to his belt. After a while, he had heard so many stories and stuffed them into that pouch so tightly that he had to push hard to get another to fit in. To make sure the stories did not escape, he tied the opening of the pouch securely with an extra rope.

The years passed, and the boy grew into a handsome young man ready to marry. A wife was chosen for him, and the entire household bustled about preparing for the young master's new wife. A faithful servant who had been with the family since the boy was born was tending to the hearth in the kitchen. He became aware of voices coming from the direction of the young master's bedroom. He went to investigate and finally realized that the sounds were emanating from the forgotten pouch of stories hanging on the wall on a rusty old nail. The old servant was quite alarmed at what he heard.

"Everyone, listen to me," a voice said, "the boy's wedding is tomorrow. Since he has kept us packed in this pouch too long, making us suffer uncomfortably for such a long time, we must think of a way to take our revenge."

"I agree," replied another voice. "Tomorrow when the young man leaves by horse to bring home his bride, I shall change into bright red berries and wait for him. I will be poisonous but shall look so delicious that he will not be able to resist plucking me and eating me. When he does, I shall kill him."

"If that doesn't work," spoke up a third voice, "I shall become a bubbling spring of water with a lovely gourd dipper floating in me. When he sees me, he will be thirsty and drink me. When I get inside him, I will make him sick, and he shall suffer day and night.

A fourth voice chided: "If you fail, then I will become a red-hot iron skewer hiding in a bag for him to step on when he dismounts at his bride's home. When he steps on me, I shall scorch his feet."

A fifth and final voice hissed: "If that too fails, I shall become poisonous snakes, thin as threads and hide in the bridal chamber. When the bride and groom have gone to sleep, I shall come out and bite them."

Greatly disturbed by all the voices, the servant took it upon himself to protect the young master. Early the next morning when the wedding procession was ready to set forth, the groom mounted his horse. Immediately the faithful, old servant came rushing out and grabbed the horse's bridle.

The old master of the house told him: "You have other work to do. You should stay and mind the house."

"No, I must lead the horse on this important day."

Because the servant was so insistent, the master finally relented and consented to let him lead the horse to the bride's home.

As the procession progressed along the winding road, the bridegroom saw there were many bright berries growing along the road. They looked so delicious.

"Stop the horse, and pick me some of those berries," the bridegroom called out.

But the servant would not stop. Instead he made the horse hurry faster, replying, "Those will stain your fine *hanbok**. Just be patient for there will be much feasting later."

Later they came upon a bubbling spring of clear water. There was even a gourd dipper floating on the water.

"Scoop me up some water," the bridegroom said to the servant. "I am very thirsty."

Again the servant cracked the whip and caused the horse to go faster. "Once we get into the shade, your thirst will soon disappear. We must not dawdle and stop every step of the way for we have many people waiting for your arrival on this most important day."

This put the young master in a bad mood, but the servant gritted his teeth and made the horse trot faster.

In record time they reached the bride's home where there was already a crowd of people gathered. The servant led the horse to the bag of chaff. As the bridegroom put out his foot to dismount, the servant pretended to fall, and shoved the bridegroom to keep him from stepping on the bag.

The bridegroom fell to the straw mats laid out on the ground. He was embarrassed, but he could not rebuke the servant in front of the guests. He bit his tongue and entered the bride's home.

After the ceremonies, the newly married couple returned to the groom's home. When night fell, the bride and groom retired to their room.

The faithful servant hid himself under the veranda outside the bridal chamber with sword in hand. As soon as they turned out the lights and settled into bed, the servant tore open the door of the room and barged inside.

The newlyweds screamed, "Who is there?" then bolted out of bed.

"Young master," the servant replied, "I cannot explain right now. Just hurry, and get out of the way." The servant plucked off the bedding with his sword then lifted the mattress. Hundreds of string snakes slithered, writhed, and coiled. The servant sliced and slashed them until all were killed.

Finally he let out a huge sigh of relief and told the couple the story of how he heard the voices from the story pouch.

So, my dear friends, that is why when you hear stories you must never store them away for they may become mean and spiteful. Stories are meant to be shared so that as many people as possible can enjoy them.

Storyteller's Notes

Hanbok is the traditional Korean dress.

I have told this story at storytelling workshops to help encourage people to speak up! Go ahead, and tell your stories! Of course, this is not to encourage repeating and spreading gossip-type stories—but good, wholesome stories. In telling stories, one can help assimilate the meaning into one's life and can help others with the lessons of the story as well as entertain.

A Tale for Sale

Master Shin lived very far from the city. He lived so far away in the country that his children and grandchildren could not visit very often. Even though Master Shin and his wife were very rich, they were also very lonely and bored. They had so much money and wealth that their brass-bound chests were overflowing with cash, and they had to bury some strings of coins in *kimchee** jars in the garden. But money does not buy happiness.

In the olden days it was not unusual to have poets and storytellers as well as other vendors come to people's doors and sell their wares. But Master Shin and his wife lived so far from the beaten path that no one dropped in on them just passing by.

Finally one day Master Shin was so bored that he gave his gate-keeper 100 strings of coins to buy a story.

"Do not return 'til you have a good story. You may pay up to 100 strings of coins for the story."

Now, this gatekeeper did not know the difference between a good story or bad. He just set out to obey his master and buy a story.

The gatekeeper had walked quite a few miles when he came to a farmer working out in his large field. The farmer greeted him warmly.

"What brings you to this part of the country in such fine clothes?"

"Master Shin sent me to buy a tale to take back to him," replied the gatekeeper.

Now the farmer was not a learned man either and didn't know how to tell stories, but he was in great need of money. He remembered that his mother had told him some stories when he was very young, but he had forgotten all of them. He could not think of a single story.

"How much are you willing to pay for a story?" the farmer inquired out of curiosity.

"Up to 100 strings of cash," the gatekeeper replied. This peaked the farmer's interest and got the wheels turning in his head. He decided he had better make up a story for this was too good an opportunity to pass by.

"I will tell you a story!" said the farmer eagerly. The gatekeeper was all too willing to be finished with his mission and return, so he agreed to listen. The farmer's blood raced. He had to think quickly. As his eyes cast about his surroundings, he spotted a stork picking its way through the rice field. The farmer spoke out loud the first thing that popped into his mind—namely, the actions of the stork.

"Step by step he comes nearer and nearer."

The gatekeeper, thinking the farmer had begun his story, repeated the words so that he could memorize it to repeat to his master.

"Step by step he comes nearer and nearer."

At that moment the stork heard something and stopped to see what it was.

"Now he stops to look! Now he stops to listen!" the farmer chanted to the unsuspecting gatekeeper.

"Now he stops to look! Now he stops to listen!" repeated the gatekeeper intently. Encouraged by this, the farmer continued watching and repeating the stork's every move.

"He bends down! He creeps!"

Again the gatekeeper repeated with great care: "He bends down! He creeps!"

Then there was a quick movement in the rice field, and a fox raised its nose into sight. With a leap the stork spread its wings and flew to safety.

"He's off! He's fleeing. Soon he will be safe!" cried the farmer.

"He's off! He's fleeing. Soon he will be safe!" mimicked the gatekeeper. Then there was a long pause. "Is that all?"

"That is all," the farmer said, chuckling to himself as he loaded the 100 strings of cash onto his own *chigye* (an A-frame carrier).

On his way home, the gatekeeper repeated over and over the story and was quite proud of himself that he had not forgotten a single word. That fact that he didn't understand the story did not concern him.

Master Shin and his wife thought it a very strange tale for they could not make any sense of it. Night after night the old man repeated it out loud word for word over and over, all the while puzzling over it. He thought it must be a riddle.

One such night when Master Shin was reciting the words carefully, a wicked man came to rob the old couple. The robber stealthily climbed over the wall and was making his way toward the house when he heard a voice say, "Step by step he comes nearer and nearer!"

This stopped the thief in his tracks, and he held his breath.

"Now he stops to look! Now he stops to listen!"

The thief looked and, seeing that the old man's back was turned to him, continued to creep toward the light that shone through the window.

"He bends down! He creeps!"

Again the thief stopped, wondering, How can the old man know everything I do? He thought that this must be a haunted house and decided to run back to safety.

"He's off! Soon he will be safe!" the old man concluded the story.

That thief ran as fast as he could and did not stop 'til he was in town with his brother thieves. All those wicked men shook their heads at the story that the frightened thief told them, and none of them ever again tried to rob the house of old Master Shin who bought the farmer's tale for 100 strings of cash!

Storyteller's Notes

*Kimchee is any pickled vegetable. Some kimchee is peppery hot and garlicky with anchovy flavor, and still others are more sweet or sour.

The coins of Korea used to have square or round holes in the center. When it was changed to no holes, the elders wondered how the coins were able to "see." Thus, one can understand how they could have had a "string of coins." But to think the gatekeeper paid 100 strings for a story is very pricey indeed!

This is a good story for audience participation. Have the audience repeat the story that the farmer recites. Then repeat after the gatekeeper as Master Shin's voice.

Another version of this story is that the gatekeeper along his journey receives one sentence from each person he meets and decides that it is a story to repeat back to his master. This would be a wonderful story to act out or read aloud as reader's theatre.

Section V

Tiger Tales

Painting by Kim Eui Kyoo, Ansan City, South Korea.

The Tiger's Grave

A boy was born into a wealthy family, but when his father died, the fortune quickly dissipated. The boy and his mother became so poor they had to move to a little shack. When the boy matured to manhood, he could not afford to get married even though he was very honest and hardworking. Still, he accepted his fate and was a dutiful son and took good care of his mother in her old age.

One day his sick and failing mother called him to her bedside saying: "My dear son, I hear that there is a very good doctor in the village of Unbong. I am certain that he can ease my pain. Please get some healing herbs from him."

There was no money for the medicine, but the son could not refuse his suffering mother. So for the first time in his life he borrowed some money from his neighbors and went to the other side of the mountain to find the doctor. He arrived just as the sun was setting, so he quickly described his mother's illness to the doctor, paid for the medicine, and set off for home again.

When he came to the top of the pass, he heard a commotion and was astonished to see a merchant wrestling with a large tiger. The man was hanging on to its tail so that it could not reach back and bite him. When the merchant saw the young man, he shouted to him for help. Immediately, the young man ran to his aid.

"Take hold of the tail!" shouted the merchant. "I shall get my knife and kill this beast!"

The young man dropped his medicine bag on the ground and took the tiger's tail. Once freed from the tiger, the merchant seized the medicine bag and took off as fast as he could.

The poor man's heart sank for he realized that he had lost his mother's medicine and soon his own life. When he thought of his mother and how she had cared for him as a child, he suddenly got a rush of energy, and he clung to the tiger's tail. But his energy gradually diminished, his hands were blistered, and his legs buckled under him. Finally as the tiger breathed into his face and then roared a triumphant roar, the man collapsed in a dead faint.

You can imagine his astonishment when he gained consciousness and found he was not harmed in any way. Since the tiger had disappeared, the young man got up and scurried down the mountain. About a mile down the trail he was surprised to find his medicine bag along the wayside. He was about to pick it up when he was horrified to see a stump of a man's arm alongside it, and further in the bushes he spied the bloody remains of a body. He was sure it was the merchant who had cheated him. The tiger must have done this to punish him for his bad deeds.

When the lad arrived home, he boiled the herbs for his mother, and in a few days her pain went away. The story of the son's devotion to his mother and the treacherous adventure with the tiger was known throughout the village, and he was much respected as a faithful son.

A few months later, he was cutting wood in the hills near home when he heard gunshots fired close by. Suddenly a tiger burst in the clearing where he was chopping. The tiger stopped, panted, then he slumped down on the ground, his strength clearly spent.

The lad looked closely at the beast and recognized it as the same one that had killed the merchant several weeks before. Grateful to the tiger for his help, he hid the tiger inside a pile of logs. When the hunters came, he misdirected them down into the valley below. After all was calm, the tiger came out from his hiding place, nodded its head three times as if in gratitude, then bounded up the hillside.

One evening a few days later, the lad and his mother had just finished dinner when they happened to look out the window and see the tiger carrying a young girl on its back. The tiger then let her down gently and bounded away into the trees.

The young man carried the girl into the house, and his mother nursed the girl back to consciousness. She then was able to tell her story.

"All I remember is that I was brushing my hair getting ready for bed when a huge tiger leaped through my window. I fainted at the sight of the beast, and when I came to, you two were tending to me."

Her parents were immediately informed of her safety, and since the young couple had fallen in love, they gave their consent to the marriage. The kidnapped girl and her rescuer lived happily in their humble home for many years.

A few years later the tiger appeared once again in their yard. It pawed the ground and swung its tail slowly from side to side. Then it lay down and died. The man buried it in the ground that bore its paw marks.

Curiously, from that day on the man's fortunes changed, and he became one of the wealthiest men in the province. After the tiger's death, a persimmon tree suddenly sprang up out of the grave and produced the most succulent fruit.

Storyteller's Notes

The tiger is the national symbol of Korea and embodies all the attributes of the Korean people. The tiger is an awesome power to be dealt with, yet can be tamed to be gentle and playful. The tiger in Korean folk literature can change into a human and back into a tiger. Sometimes the tiger takes on the form of a spiritual monk and helps people. Tigers are also shown to be discerning of human inner character and will only eat or harm those who are not of good character.

It is also said that some people are so evil that even tigers will not stoop to eat them.

You may read much more about the Korean perception of the tiger in Kathleen J. Crane Foundation's book, *Tiger, Burning Bright: More Myths Than Truths About Korean Tigers.*

The Tiger's Eyebrow Hair

Farmer Sok was an extremely good-natured man. There was not an evil bone or thought in his body. Unfortunately, he was as poor as he was good. Although he worked hard from sunup to sundown, he many times had to skip meals. He nevertheless worked diligently every day in the hopes that his luck would change.

His wife of forty had not produced any children, and to make the burden even worse, she was ill-tempered and coldhearted. She screamed and yelled ugly, abusive words at him, bemoaning their conditions though she was unwilling to lift a finger to help. Instead of sharing the bowl of soup with him, she ate it all herself and insulted his inability to provide for her.

"You are worthless. How can you stand to live with yourself? You may as well kill yourself and be done with all your troubles. I can't stand to live like this any longer with you and your mangy dog. Get out of my house!" And she shoved him out the door.

The moon shone brightly, but Sok took no notice. He felt like he wanted to die. He was so despondent and weary he just wandered about. When his stomach grumbled, he had a vague sense that he would like to find something to eat, but he wondered where and how he would pay for it. Sok finally decided to spend the night at Tiger Rock. It was said that in ancient times a tiger used to come and cry at this rock every first full moon of the year. On this night he felt like crying there himself.

As he sat on the rock, he sighed deeply again and again. Sometimes a tear rolled down his cheek and glistened in the moonlight. Then a rustling sound in the bushes caught his attention. Sok looked up and saw an old monk with long, white hair sitting near a tree, picking lice out of his clothes and popping them into his mouth. First he thought that he might be a ghost, but then he wondered if the monk were in the same situation he was in, so he cautiously approached the monk and asked, "Pardon me, but why are you out in the woods at this time of night?"

The monk slowly looked up and replied: "What I am doing here is my business. The question is, What are you doing here?"

So Sok told him his life story and how his wife threw him out that night. "I have no wish to live with her or to live at all now."

The monk smiled sympathetically at him and then pulled out a hair from his eyebrow and gave it to Sok. "Hold this up to your eye."

When Sok did as he was told, he was astonished at what he saw. Instead of the old monk, there was a huge tiger with his mouth wide-open and ready to devour him. Sok immediately threw the hair down from his eye, and there was the smiling old monk again.

"Yes, I am actually a tiger. I came out this way for a walk when I became hungry. Don't be afraid, for you must know that tigers are spiritual creatures. You are a true human, so I can't eat you. It's only those so-called humans that are actually pigs and dogs and other lowlifes that we tigers can eat. There really are few humans in this world.

"For instance, your wife. The only thing she has ever given you is a miserable life. She could either be a pig or possibly a dog. Take this hair from my eyebrow, and go back to your house. Look at your wife through it. If she turns out to be an animal, go right away to Aji Village. There you will find a widow living in a hut under a tall pine tree. Tell her what I just told you, and take her as your new wife. I promise you that you will prosper and be happy with her."

Sok thanked the monk and started back to his house. He looked back once to watch the monk, but he had already turned himself back into a tiger. The tiger pounced on a man coming out of the woods and carried him off. At this you can imagine how fast Sok hightailed it out of there!

As soon as he returned home, he looked at his wife through the hair of the tiger's eyebrow. He saw a fat, sleeping sow, slobbering and snorting and having a bad dream.

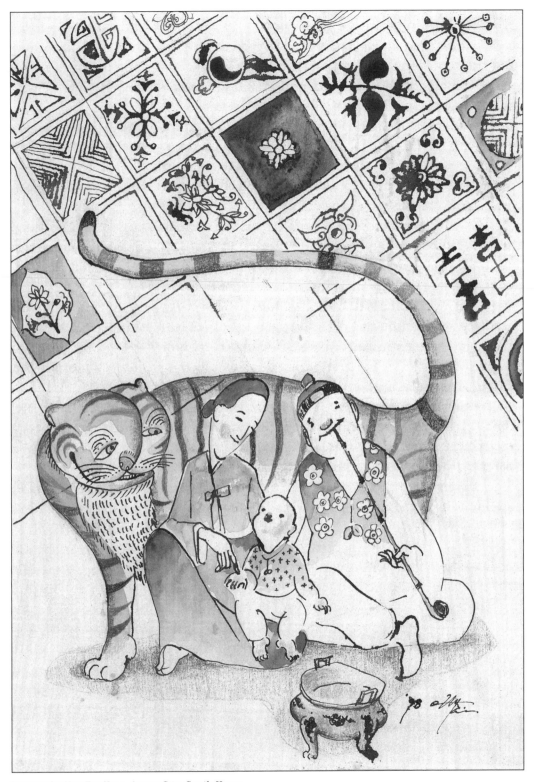

Painting by Kim Eui Kyoo, Ansan City, South Korea.

The Tiger's Eyebrow Hair

Sok didn't even stop to say good-bye and took off for Aji Village. He walked for three days and finally arrived at the hut under the pine trees that the monk told him to look for. He called several times for someone to come to the door, but there was no response. Finally, he pushed open the gate and went in. He found a woman sleeping.

She was awakened when the floor creaked under his weight, and she screamed: "Who are you? How dare you enter a house without permission!"

Sok begged forgiveness, and then he explained what the monk had instructed him to do. The woman finally understood and welcomed him. Then she told him her story.

"After I got married, life turned rotten. My husband was unfaithful, always out every night with a different girl. Then one day he disappeared and never returned."

"It looks like we're both in the same boat now."

"It is curious," the woman started to recall. "Just as you came in I was dreaming that some old man with a white beard and glowing face told me that a stranger would come and be my true husband. He went on to say that if I honored and served him well, I would have a happy life. The old man disappeared, and as soon as I awoke, there you were."

Sok and the woman were married and lived in her house. They worked hard together side by side. She soon gave birth to a healthy baby boy, which added to their joy. They did indeed have a happy life together all the rest of their days.

A Tiger by the Tail

A young man started on his journey to Seoul to take the civil-service examination. The path was very long and difficult. After walking for many miles through the dense forest, he decided to sit down and rest his aching feet. He sat down on a broken log and smoked his pipe.

After a while he decided to resume his journey and felt around for his walking stick. Suddenly his hand felt something slithery. He looked down, and to his utter terror he found himself grasping the tail of a tiger. The tiger had been sleeping, hidden by the very rock he had sat upon.

The tiger awoke and gave a tremendous growl. The man was frozen with fear yet kept his wits, for he knew he must hold on to the tail or else the tiger might attack him. The tiger continued to roar louder and tried to attack, but the man held on for his life and kept the tiger at bay. The man cried for help, but no one was near enough to hear.

After quite some time, when the man thought that he could not hold on any longer, he spotted a monk walking by, so he yelled to him. When the monk reached him, the man pleaded for help.

"Take my walking stick, and kill the tiger before he kills me!"

"I cannot kill a living thing," replied the monk. "It is against my beliefs."

The man pleaded and begged, but the monk would not make one move to kill the tiger. Then the man had an idea.

Painting by Kim Eui Kyoo, Ansan City, South Korea.

"If you hold the tiger's tail, then I can kill the tiger," he suggested. The monk thought about this a while. When he realized that he would not actually be killing the tiger himself, he agreed to hold the tiger's tail.

Finally the man was able to let go of the tiger's tail. Greatly relieved, the man massaged his tired hands, picked up his walking stick, and started to leave. Now it was the monk's turn to be anxious and fearful.

"You can kill the tiger now," he reminded the man.

"Oh, no. I cannot kill a living thing. It is against my beliefs," replied the free man. Then he left the monk holding the tiger's tail.

Storyteller's Notes

Most stories are favorable to Buddhism and monks, but I have found several stories in Korean literature making fun of the Buddhist; for example, the bad husband receives a procession of priests who demand money to rebuild their temple of Buddha in "The Good Brother's Reward" in Frances Carpenter's *Tales of a Korean Grandmother*. Another example is my next story, adapted from "The Salt Peddler and the Monk," in Kathleen Crane Foundation's book *Tiger, Burning Bright*. There was a time when corruption was so widespread among Buddhist monks that they were not respected. These kinds of stories serve to remind us that while the teachings may be very righteous, it is hard for humans to follow—hence the saying, "The spirit is willing, but the flesh is weak" from the Judeo-Christian Bible.

Art by Brian Barry.

Another Tiger by the Tail

This story will show you how perilous it can be to be on foot in the steep and densely wooded mountains of Kangwon Province. There was once upon a time a salt peddler who had to travel over the highest pass. After climbing to the top with great difficulty, he removed his A-frame carrier from his back and sat down on a tree trunk to catch his breath.

Immediately a huge tiger jumped out from behind a tree. In a huge panic equal to the size of the tiger, the man grabbed hold of the tiger's tail. He had heard that a tiger cannot bend back around, so it was helpless as long as the man could hold on to the tail. The tiger strained and twisted to get free, but the peddler held on with superhuman strength.

Soon a young monk came up the pass. When the peddler saw the monk, he thought that he felt the hand of Providence watching over him. As he struggled to hold on to the tiger, he called to the monk, "Come here, and help me!"

"I am your humble servant," replied the monk, approaching, but keeping a respectable distance from the lurching tiger.

"As you can see I have my hands full. I am trying to subdue this tiger, but it will take some time. As luck would have it, I must relieve myself. Please do me the favor of holding this tail while I do my business. Then we'll kill the thing and share the profits from selling the skin."

Painting by Kim Eui Kyoo, Ansan City, South Korea.

The monk then thought Buddha was watching over him and smiled broadly. "As you wish, sir." He grabbed the tiger's tail. "Go ahead and relieve yourself. Don't worry, I will hold on 'til you get back."

The peddler immediately ran into the trees, forgetting his A-frame and pack. He just kept running to get as far away from the tiger as possible, thinking all the while that "a monk's fate is no business of mine."

But the peddler's conscience started to bother him over the years. Finally after three years it bothered him so badly that he climbed back to the pass where he had left the monk. On the way up, he fretted that the tiger might be waiting for him, or the monk's ghost would do him harm. Yet when he reached the place, there was the monk still holding the same tiger by the tail, just as he was three years before.

"What are you two doing here after all this time?"

"After you went to relieve yourself," the monk groaned as the tiger jerked hard, "the tiger began to lunge and pull even harder, so there was nothing I could do but to let it drag me along. I have been all over eight provinces several times like this and just got back a few minutes ago. If you had taken longer, you would have missed us because we would have been off on our fourth tour. Here, please take the tail back!"

As the peddler stood there dumbfounded, the tiger lunged at him. So he took out his knife and killed the tiger. Then he and the monk skinned the tiger and took the skin to the market.

After receiving a handsome sum, they split the money between them. The peddler had enough money to support himself and stop peddling salt for a living. And the monk could afford to grow his hair back and live the life of a normal person since he no longer wanted to be a monk.

Section VI

Tall Tales

The Wealthy Miser

In the town of Chinju lived a wealthy miser by the name of Choe. One day his son married Ae-hyun and brought her home to live with them.

Ae-hyun could not believe her eyes and ears. Her father-in-law would run around and around the courtyard before every meal and sit down to the table breathless. When she inquired why, he proudly informed her, "If you run until it hurts, you forget what the taste of food is and are satisfied with eating just rice with a drop of soy sauce."

Not too long after she moved in with the Choe family, Mr. Choe noticed a fly on the rim of the soy-sauce bowl.

"You horrible insect! You are stealing my soy sauce. I will kill you for that!" he roared, chasing the fly around the room. "I could eat a whole bowl of rice with the two drops of soy sauce you took, and you would rob me of that. I'll not let you get away with it!" He finally caught the fly and chewed it up so as to get all the soy sauce out of its body.

Ae-hyun and all the household were ashamed and intimidated by his meanness. Ae-hyun was not used to eating meals without meat or vegetables and on this day she could take it no longer. She called to a fishmonger who was passing by the house and asked to look at his fish. He was surprised, having never sold any to this household before. Ae-hyun picked up every fish

and asked him how much each one was. She tried to bargain one fish down but to no avail. Finally she stomped back into the house, saying she would not buy any. The fishmonger was also very angry and disgusted with her for wasting his time.

Ae-hyun walked into the kitchen and had the cooks carefully pour water over her hands into the soup pot, making sure all the fish scales went into the soup. That night there was a pot of fish soup at the dinner table.

Master Choe was enraged, "Who bought this fish?"

"I did, honorable father-in-law," Ae-hyun responded.

"Who gave you permission to waste money on fish?"

"But, honorable father-in-law, I did not spend a dime. I only touched all the fish, and then washed off the scales into the soup pot to make this tasty fish soup," she explained, beaming with pride and thinking that she had finally figured out how to please both herself and the father-in-law.

"What a waste!" he raged. "If you had washed your hands in the well, we would have had fish soup for months!"

Storyteller's Notes

Audiences love the stories with humor. They especially like tall tales. One definition of a tall tale is a story that gets more and more ridiculous! These kinds of stories people remember. They may like all the other stories for their poignancy and adventure, but people always come to me and recite the tall tales back to me or continue to tell these stories to others. Every culture has their tall tales—the humor is universal. It is a wonderful way to illustrate a point because as the point is repeated, it gets bigger and bigger and is taken to its logical conclusion. We all know people who exaggerate or who interpret rules too literally. A tall tale can demonstrate the folly of excesses.

The Charming Flute

There once was a woodcutter who played a Korean flute with such great skill that he was able to express his every mood with the flute. He played soulful sounds when he was mourning a loss. He played soothing sounds to calm people and put them to sleep. But mostly he was a happy person and played joyful and merry tunes. He liked to play his flute wherever he went, especially as he went to the forest to chop wood. As he played, the birds flocked around him and harmonized with him. Children gathered around him and sang and danced as he played in the meadow.

He was in a fine, playful mood one day when he was rudely confronted by a large, ferocious tiger. Just before the tiger leaped toward him, the man spotted a tall tree and scrambled up it as fast as he could. The tiger tried to climb the tree after him but was not able to. It tried several times but finally gave up and disappeared into the thick forest.

The woodcutter was much relieved but was still in such a state of shock that he was not able to come down out of the tree. He just sat there trying to calm himself. Soon the tiger returned with several other tigers to help him capture the man.

One tiger stood next to the tree while a second climbed on top of him, then a third climbed on top of the second. The fourth tiger climbed on top of the tower of tigers and was within reach of the poor woodcutter.

Painting by Kim Eui Kyoo, Ansan City, South Korea.

The Charming Flute

At this the woodcutter decided to accept his fate and die happily and joyfully. So he took up his flute and began to play the merriest tune he had ever played. The tiger on the bottom happened to be very musical and loved to dance to music. He swayed and pranced to the rhythm. As he danced, the other tigers struggled to keep balance, but they quickly tumbled down, and the whole tower toppled over.

Noticing what was happening, the woodcutter played faster and faster. When all the tigers except the dancing tiger had fallen to the ground unconscious, the woodcutter quietly slipped down from the tree and ran into the village still playing his flute. He only stopped playing when he knew he was safe. And thus, the woodcutter's life was saved by his charming flute.

Storyteller's Notes

This story serves to illustrate how the power of music can influence and intoxicate. Music is truly a universal language and a necessary seasoning to life. Many people have been led afar or astray by music. There are studies that conclude that even plants are influenced in their growth by the music that is played. Remember the "Pied Piper of Hamelin" and how he was able to drive the rats out of town!

Reflections

A very long time ago Mr. Pak lived with his family high in the mountains. None of his family ever ventured into the city and so were not affected by the modern inventions. They heard many rumors of strange things, but they dared not go.

Curiosity got the better of Mr. Pak, and after many months of planning he decided to go into Hanyang, the nation's capital, to explore. This caused quite a stir with his parents and wife, but he would not be dissuaded.

Although the trip was long and hard, Mr. Pak thought the trip well worth the effort when he finally arrived in the city. The sights, sounds, and smells were quite exciting to him. He found so many different kinds of trinkets that could be purchased. The object that intrigued him the most was a small piece of glass with a frame inlaid with abalone shells that he could look into and see his reflection.

After several days he purchased a few things for his family and mirror for himself and started on his journey back home.

When he arrived home, he had so much to relate to everyone about all the things he saw and did in Hanyang but never once mentioned the mirror. He put it away in his special box of treasures. Almost weekly he took it out to look at himself.

One day his wife happened to come into the room without his knowing. She saw him looking at something and smiling. "What is that?" she asked.

"Nothing! Nothing at all!" he said a little too emphatically as he quickly put something back into his box. "I was just thinking I should get back to hoeing the garden."

When she was sure he was busy outside, she opened the box. "I wonder what this is," she said as she picked up the mirror. After turning it over and over she held up the shiny side to her face for a closer look. "Who is this? That man has brought home a pretty, young girl!"

She was so angry that she took the mirror to her mother-in-law and told her what had just happened. "Let me see," said the mother-in-law, taking the mirror and holding it up to her face. "This isn't a pretty, young woman. It's an old, wrinkled hag! Why would he do that?"

"No, Mother. He brought home a pretty, young girl! I saw her myself."

"No, it's an old woman!"

They argued back and forth, screeching louder and louder until the father-in-law came into the room to investigate.

"What is all this noise about? Why are you fighting?"

"Father, maybe you can settle this argument. I found this small, flat, shiny thing Husband brought from Hanyang. I looked into it—"

"She says he has a pretty, young woman in it," interrupted the mother-in-law, "but all I can see is an old woman, and I can't figure out why he would want her."

"Give it to me so I can take a look." As the father-in-law looked into it he laughed. "What are you talking about, there's only a wrinkled, old man." Then he frowned, puzzled. "Let's leave it right here until my son comes in to explain this."

Meanwhile, the couple's four-year-old boy came in and caught sight of the shiny object on the table. When he looked into it, he was startled to see a boy staring back at him. He stuck his tongue out and the other boy stuck out his tongue. He frowned, and the other did the same.

He got up and ran outside crying. "He took my ball. . . ."

"Don't cry!" A teenager came running over from across the street. "Who took your ball?"

"He did!" replied the little boy and handed the teenager the mirror.

The teenager looked into the mirror and scowled. "You big bully! I'll teach you to pick on little kids!" he shouted and hit the "bully" with his fist. *Chaeng!* The mirror broke into dozens of shards and fell to the ground.

The First to Be Served

It was New Year's Day, the most important day of the year, and Toad, Hare, and Deer arrived at the festivities. When dinnertime came, there arose the question of who was to be served first, since it is customary to serve the oldest first.

"I am the oldest," spoke up Deer, proudly tossing his antlers. "I should be served first."

"You may be the biggest, but that doesn't mean you are the oldest. I am sure that I am, so I must be served first," retorted Hare.

"Stop your arguing," admonished Toad. "Please explain why you think you are the oldest instead of just claiming to be the oldest."

"I'm so old that I nailed the stars in the sky," replied Deer.

Hare snickered, amused. "I am the one who planted the tree from which the ladder was made that you used to nail the stars to the sky. That would make me your grandfather."

Then Toad started to weep. Deer and Hare looked over at him confused and asked him why he was crying.

"Well, listening to the two of you made me sad," explained Toad. "I once had three sons, and each planted a tree. The first used his tree to make

Art by Brian Barry.

the handle of the hammer you used to nail the stars to the sky. The second used his tree to make the plow that was used to dig the furrow for the Silvery Stream (Milky Way). And the third used his tree to make an awl to bore the holes for the stars. But all three died before their tasks were finished. So what you said made me sentimental about my sons who died so long ago." Hare and Deer were silenced by what they heard, and Toad was honored by being served his dinner first.

Storyteller's Notes

It is considered polite in Korea to ask or volunteer one's age because age has many privileges. The old custom is to add a year to your age on your first, sixtieth, and eightieth birthdays, plus—a person is considered one year old at birth. The advantage is that in Asian countries, people don't feel useless and obsolete in old age as in the West and, hence, maintain their vitality.

References

Korean Cultural Center

The Korean Cultural Center

The Korean Cultural Center (KCC) serves the general Los Angeles public by providing information about and performances of Korean culture. Operated by the Korean government's Ministry of Culture and Tourism, the KCC charges no fees for its services. Its Wilshire Boulevard facility contains a museum collection of replicas of several of Korea's most important artifacts, a gallery for modern art, a library of materials about Korea (in both English and Korean), and a film and video lending center. The KCC sponsors occasional events where the public can view professional Korean artists for free. It also runs a series of free classes and workshops on various forms of Korean cultural expressions: music, dance, folk art, and language.

Korean Cultural Center
5505 Wilshire Blvd.
Los Angeles, CA 90036
Tel: (213) 936-7141
Fax: (213) 936-5712
Homepage: http://www.kccla.org
Hours: Monday-Friday 9:00 a.m. to 5:00 p.m.
Saturday 10:00 a.m. to 1:00 p.m.
Closed Sundays and Korean and American holidays

Bibliography

Adams, Edward B. *The Birth of Tangun*. Seoul: Seoul International Publishing House, 1986.

———. *Korean Folk Story for Children Series I, II, III, IV, and V*. Seoul: International Publishing House, 1981.

Carpenter, Frances. *Tales of a Korean Grandmother*. Seoul: Tuttle, 1973.

Cole, Joanna. *Bestloved Folktales of the World*. Garden City, NY: Doubleday, 1982.

Conger, David. *Many Lands and Many Stories, Asian Folktales for Children*. Tokyo: Charles E. Tuttle, 1987.

Courlander, Harold. *The Tiger's Whisker, and Other Tales and Legends from Asia and the Pacific*. New York: Harcourt, Brace and Company, 1959.

Crane, Kathleen J., Foundation. *Tiger, Burning Bright: More Myths Than Truths About Korean Tigers*. Seoul: Hollym International Corp., 1992.

Han, Suzanne Crowder. *Korean Folk and Fairy Tales*. Korea: Hollym, 1991.

———. *The Rabbit's Escape*. New York: Henry Holt, 1995.

———. *The Rabbit's Judgment*. New York: Henry Holt, 1994.

Im, Bang, and Yi Ryuk. *Korean Folk Tales, Imps, Ghosts, and Fairies*. Tokyo: Charles E. Tuttle, 1986.

Kim, So-un. *The Story Bag, A Collection of Korean Folk Tales*. Tokyo: Charles E. Tuttle, 1960.

Lee, Jai Hyon. *Korean Lore*. Seoul: Office of Public Information, 1953.

Ministry of Culture and Information. *Korean Folk Stories for Children*, 5 audio cassette tapes each Vol. 1 and 2. Korea: Samseong, 1986.

O'Brien, Anne Sibley. *The Princess and the Beggar: A Korean Folktale*. New York: Scholastic, 1993.

Park, Yongjun. *Traditional Tales of Old Korea: A Mixture of Legend and History of Korea's Colorful Past*, 5 vol. Seoul: Hanguk Munhwa, 1974.

Riordan, James. *Korean Folktales*. Oxford: Oxford University Press, 1994.

Seros, Kathleen. *Sun and Moon, Fairy Tales from Korea*. Korea: Hollym, 1982.

Yu, Chai-Shin. *Korean Folk Tales*. Toronto, Ontario: Kensington Educational, 1986.

Zong, In-sob. *Folk Tales from Korea*. New York: Grove Press, 1979.

Index

Biographies of Author, Editor, and Artists

Lindy Soon Curry has been studying and performing stories throughout the United States since 1990. She was the 1995 recipient of Colorado's "Asian Woman of Achievement Award" in the Arts and Culture category for her performances of Asian folktales. She enjoys performing for audiences of all ages because folktales well told can bridge the generation gap as well as be the catalyst for healing in many relationships.

Dr. Chan E. Park is assistant professor of Korean language and literature at Ohio State University. She is also a performer and researcher of *p'ansori*, a traditional Korean storytelling art of stylized singing. In her numerous talks and performances around the nation and abroad, Dr. Park not only introduces Korean culture to her audiences but helps rekindle intellectual and public interest in storytelling, a powerful yet intimate tool of cultural and philosophical education.

A native of Massachusetts, **Brian Barry** is a long-term resident of Korea, a professional translator and writer, a Dharma teacher, and Buddhist artist since 1986. You may read excerpts of his upcoming book, *The "Goldfish" Buddhist Art Tradition in Korea*, on his website: www.designpark.co.kr/bbbudart.

Kim Eui Kyoo teaches drawing at Kay Won School of Art and Design in Korea and has had many exhibitions in Korea and America. His works include religious art, sculpture, print-making, book illustration, and other art forms. In this book, his illustrations were done with color pencil and watercolor used on ground paper preprinted with mixed gesso. His illustrations incorporate the traditional Korean sensibility of the humanistic spirit, rather than the confrontational concept of evil and good.